DATE DUE

W9-ABK-734

Look Back and See

Look Back and See

Twenty Lively Tales for Gentle Tellers

by Margaret Read MacDonald

Illustrations by Roxane Murphy

The H. W. Wilson Company
1991

For my father, Murray Read,
who has a story for every situation
and eighty-eight years of experience in telling them.

Library of Congress Cataloging-in-Publication Data

MacDonald, Margaret Read, 1940–
    Look back and see : twenty lively tales for gentle tellers / by
Margaret Read MacDonald ; illustrations by Roxane Murphy.
    p. cm.
Includes bibiolgraphical references.
ISBN 0-8242-0810-2 : $35.00
    1. Storytelling. 2. Libraries, Children's—Activity programs.
I. Murphy, Roxane. II. Title.
Z718.3M23 1991
027.62'51—dc20   91-2539

ACKNOWLEDGMENTS

Thanks to Peter Johnson and Jennifer MacDonald for reading these tales aloud to test their oral quality. Their keen ear helped in the final editing stages.

Thanks to Michelle Gabrielle for presenting me with several fine folktale collections from her travels in the U.S.S.R. "Grandfather Bear is Hungry" and "Tiny Mouse Goes Traveling" grew from that gift; Kirsten Mueller for sharing Australian tale collections, including "Why Koala has no Tail"; Martha Eshelman Smith for tale-note suggestions; Peter Johnson, Winnifred Jaeger, and Mary K. Whittington for help with musical notation; Hildred Ides and the Makah Cultural and Research Center for permission to use "The Elk and the Wren"; and all the Seattle audiences who helped shape these tales!

And special thanks to my editors. To Bruce Carrick for his constant support of my work. And to Judy O'Malley, whose enthusiasm for this project spurred me on, and whose incessant attention to detail made certain that everything came out right.

CONTENTS

For other singing tales, see "Quail Song" (page 121), "The Singing Turtle" (page 137), "The Teeny Weeny Bop" (page 147), "Tiny Mouse Goes Traveling" (page 130), "Turkey Girl" (page 45), and "The Elk and the Wren" (page 103).

AUDIENCE PARTICIPATION

Most of the tales in this book have audience-participation possibilities.

TEACHING TALES

Also see "Whole Language Uses" (page 166) and "Character Traits" (page 171).

CONTENTS

TALES FOR QUIET MOMENTS

TALES WITH IMPROVISATIONAL SLOTS

PART II: SUGGESTED USES AND SOURCES

INTRODUCTION

When selecting tales to tell, my own penchant is for the rowdy trickster, who often proves quite amoral. The boisterous flow of such finely-crafted folktales as "Mr. Fox" and "The Hobyahs" blinds me to prolonged concern over their violent nature. But many of the teachers and librarians who enroll in my storytelling workshops ask for a gentler brand of story. So I began searching for tales with a milder demeanor. And I found them! Here are twenty of my favorite gentle tales. There are no amoral protagonists in this collection—or, if they are behaving wrongly at the story's start, they learn to do better before it ends.

Some of these tales have obvious morals, others do not; most have an underlying lesson. For tellers who wish to focus on a particular moral aspect or quality, a list of tales that emphasize positive and negative character traits is given on page 00. However, the criterion for inclusion in this collection was gentleness, not moral tone.

Though gentle in mood, most of these tales are actually quite spirited in the telling, with lots of the audience-participation fun that I enjoy. I have tried to choose tales that are not already in wide use among storytellers, and I think you will find many exciting new stories here.

About Tales with Improvisational Slots

I recently observed Floating Eagle Feather, a traveling storyteller, perform an improvisational story with a group of four- and five-year-olds. He allowed the children to provide almost all of the images in the tale. After it was completed, he asked if any of them wanted to tell a story. Several children volunteered; each sat on the storybench and told a brief but well-formulated story—extemporaneously! It was clear that his improvisational tale had encouraged them to believe each of them had the ability to make up a story too.

Several of the tales in this collection lend themselves to some improvised participation by the audience. These tales involve a bit of risk-taking, as at given points within the story, the teller turns certain decisions over to members of the audience. You need to be ready to think quickly on your feet in order to incorporate their suggestions (ranging from the predictable to the wild) into your performance. You also need to be confident of your control over the group's behavior before you release them into a torrent of shouted ideas or frantically waving hands. This is a very playful approach to storytelling, and tales with potential for improvisation make nice breaks within larger story programs. As Floating Eagle Feather demonstrated, they also offer an opportunity to involve the audience more fully in the story process and to inspire listeners to create and tell their own stories.

About the Tale Notes

Each teller will want to shape the story to fit a personal style. In the tale notes, I give references to help you consult other sources for the tale and make your own comparisons. Another collector may have told the tale in a way that pleases you, or you may want to add elements of another variant to this version. I have frequently included type and motif numbers to aid you in locating variations and similar stories in such indexes as Stith Thompson's *Motif-Index of Folk Literature,* Anti Aarne and Stith Thompson's *The Types of the Folktale,* and my index of children's collections, *The Storyteller's Sourcebook: A Subject, Title, and Motif Index to Folklore Collections for Children.*

The tale notes mention any significant departures from the folktale source which have crept into my version of a story through repeated tellings. I also try to indicate any potentially enjoyable bits I chose to leave out of my version, but which you may wish to include, if they excite you. It seems appropriate for new tellers to mark old tales with their own styles, but it is important to note where such changes occur.

A Note About the Sources
and Development of These Folktales

The world is alive with delightful, tellable tales. If only we could all travel to hear the master tellers of each culture performing for their friends and families, these traditions would come alive for us. We could experience the tellings firsthand and would be able to pick our favorites to bring home and retell for our own audiences. Through the centuries, stories have traveled from culture to culture in just that direct, informal way: storytellers traveled, listened, remembered, and went on to retell the tale for new audiences. Today, only a few traveling bards remain. One is Floating Eagle Feather, who makes a circuit of the world every two years, spreading tales and learning new ones as he goes. But we do have a new category of story listeners, as folklorists now travel to listen for us. Equipped with tape recorder and video camera, the folklorist records the entire story event. And today's folklorist is not only interested in the story text itself, but wants to see how the teller performs and how the audience responds. The folklorist also wants to know why these stories are told and how they function for the group. Most importantly for our purposes, the folklorist wants to write these stories down in a way that will help the reader bring them to life as closely as possible to the way the teller originally performed them. And so, we have ethnopoetic texts, created with a line break when the teller pauses in speech, and featuring various-sized typefaces to cue vocal stress and other dynamics in performance. This new use of the ethnopoetic text brings the story to the would-be teller in a much more accessible format than collections we have used previously. It is to these new ethnopoetic collections that I have turned to search out stories to share with my audiences.

I especially enjoy a form of audience-participation storytelling, which I think of as group play, and which can also move easily into group drama. Fortunately for me, this type of playful storytelling is popular in many cultures, and folklorists have recorded master tellers performing this genre. Reading through armloads of folktale collections, I make files of those tales which might be fun to tell, watching for chants, repetitive phrases, songs, places where the audience can join in the performance. Then, selecting a potentially-tellable tale from my file, I begin to play with it with various audiences. Each audience, through its response, teaches me something about the tale. As I shape the tale to please them and to please myself, it keeps changing. At some point in this process, though, each tale reaches a stable form that is consistently pleasing to its audiences. I set that tale rendition down on paper and let it rest. After a few weeks, I ask someone to read it aloud to me to see if the tale can live through a cold reading. If not, I take it back to my audiences for more polishing.

Because of the communal way in which these story scripts are developed, my desire for folkloric authenticity sometimes gives way to my joy in having the audience help shape the tale. Each telling is different, as I like to constantly play with the audience and with the tale. Before publication, I go through each story carefully, restoring any wanderings from the source that seem inappropriate. Changes that add to the tellability and joy of the tale are kept. By the time the story reaches print here, it has been modified from the folkteller's rendition. Sometimes, the changes are slight; at other times, they are considerable. I hope that the teller will understand any ways in which I may have altered these tales.

As a folklorist, I am committed to maintaining the authenticity of my source and would like to reproduce the tales exactly as they were performed by the traditional teller. But as a storyteller, I know that no tale is ever told the same way twice. Understanding that the tale belongs to the teller and to the audience, I fall easily into the spontaneous mode, which fosters adaptation. The story *must* change to live; each event recreates the vision anew. The stories in this collection are the product of the folk imagination of a southern-Indiana storyteller, performing for an audience of Seattle, Washington, children, drawing inspiration from the recorded tellings of many cultures. I hope each of you will touch them with your own imagination and spread them joyfully wherever *you* travel. Have fun playing with them!

Part I: Tales

THE SNOW BUNTING'S LULLABY

Mama and Papa Snow Bunting flew north to Siberia in the spring.

They built a nest there on the rocks.
Mama Bunting laid a tiny egg.
She fluffed her feathers and sat on that egg.
She sat and sat and then
      "peepeep . . . peepeep . . . peepeep" . . . out came a little
        chick.
At once it began to cry.

      "Peepeep . . . anhnanhnn . . . peepeep . . . anhnanhnn . . .
        peepeep . . . anhnanhnn . . ."
Mama Bunting said,
      "No no, don't cry.
      I'll sing you a lullaby."

3

She spread her wings over the nest and she sang:
>   "Whose toes are these?
>   Whose wings are these?
>   Whose eyes are these?
>   Whose head is this?"

But the baby just kept on crying.
>   "Peepeep . . . anhnanhnn . . . peepeep . . . anhnanhnn . . .
>   peepeep . . . anhnanhnn . . ."

"Let me try Mama," said Papa Bunting.
Papa Bunting spread his wings over the nest.
He sang:
>   "Whose little toes are these?
>   Whose little wings are these?
>   Whose little eyes are these?
>   Whose little head is this?

>   "Are . . . you . . . asleep?"

Papa tapped the chick gently as he asked.
And sure enough, this lullaby had put the chick to sleep.
>   "Ahmmmmmmm. . . . . ."

>   "Thank you Papa Bunting!" said Mama Bunting.
>   "I will sing that lovely song whenever our chick cries . . . .
>   And it will go right to sleep."

Papa Bunting flew off to find food for the family.
And Mama Bunting settled down on the nest.
After a while the chick woke up and began to cry again.
>   "Peepeep . . . anhnanhnn . . . peepeep . . . anhnanhnn . . .
>   peepeep . . . anhnanhnn . . ."

But Mama Bunting began at once to sing the lullaby.
>   "Whose little toes are these?

4

Whose little wings are these?
Whose little eyes are these?
Whose little head is this? . . .

Are . . . you . . . asleep?"
And the chick fell back to sleep.
"Ahmmmmmmm. . . . . ."
While Mama Bunting was singing, Kutkha the Raven flew past.
Kutkha liked that song.
He flew right down.

"Mama Bunting, give me that song.
I want to sing like that."

"Oh no, Kutkha. I must keep this song.
Papa Bunting gave it to me.
I need this lullaby to put my baby to sleep."

"Well, I am much BIGGER than you." said Kutkha.
"If you won't give it to me
I'll just TAKE it!"

Kutkha SNATCHED the song right out of Mother Bunting's beak and
flew off with it.

The baby bunting woke up and began to cry.

"peepeep . . . anhnanhnn . . . peepeep . . . anhnanhnn . . .
peepeep . . . anhnanhnn . . ."

It would not be comforted.

5

When Papa Bunting came home he said,
>"Why aren't you singing our song to the baby, Mama?
>Why is it crying?"

>"Kutkha the Raven stole our song!" said Mama Bunting.
>He snatched it right out of my beak and flew away with it."

Papa Bunting's eyes flashed and he stamped his feet.
>"We will see about THAT!
>Bring me my hunting gloves.
>Bring me my bow.
>Bring me my arrows."

Papa Bunting set off running over the snow
>looking for Kutkha the Raven.

Papa Bunting ran faster and faster.
Soon he spread his wings and began to fly over the plain
>looking for Kutkha the Raven.

Up and over the mountain he soared
>and down into a valley.

There was the raven colony.
They were sitting about in groups singing their raven song.
>"Karrr! Karrr! Karrr! Karrr!"

But over to one side Papa Bunting saw a raven sitting on top of a skin
>tent all by himself.

That Raven was nodding and humming with his eyes closed.
Every little while he would wiggle his toes.
He would flap his wings.
He would point to his eyes.
Then he would point at his head.

6

Papa Bunting crept up close and listened.
He heard that raven singing to himself.
    "Whose little toes are these?
    Whose little wings are these?
    Whose little eyes are these?
    Whose little head is this?
    Kutkha the Raven's! Huh . . . huh . . . huh . . ."
The raven was laughing at his own joke.
    "Kutkha the Raven!" called Papa Bunting.
    "You give me back my song!"

    "I'm BIGGER than you and I'll keep it myself,"
Kutkha shouted back.
    "Oh no you won't," said Papa Bunting to himself.
Papa Bunting fitted a tiny arrow in his little bow.

Kutkha began to sing
    "Whose little toes are these?"
Papa Bunting SHOT that tiny arrow.
Right at Kutkha's toes.
    "Oh. Oh. They're MY toes!" cried Kutkha.

But Kutkha went on singing.
    "Whose little wings are these?"
Papa Bunting took aim.
He shot a tiny arrow at Kutkha's wing.
    "Oh. Oh. They're MY wings!" cried Kutkha.

Kutkha wouldn't stop singing.
    "Whose little eyes are these?"
Papa Bunting shot another arrow.
    "Oh. Oh. They're MY eyes!"

7

"Whose little head is this?"
Papa Bunting shot his last arrow.
"Oh. Oh. It's MY head!
KARRR! KARRR! KARRR!"

Kutkha coughed and dropped the song.
Papa Bunting ran swiftly and grabbed the song from the snow.
"Goodbye, Kutkha!
If you want a fine song you must make it up yourself!"
Papa Bunting took the song in his beak.
He flew straight back to Mama Bunting.
"Here, Mama. Now you can sing to our chick."

Mama Bunting spread her wings over the nest.

She sang:
"Whose little toes are these?
Whose little wings are these?
Whose little eyes are these?
Whose little head is this?

Are . . . you . . . asleep?"
"Ahmmmmmmm. . . . . ." It was asleep.

NOTES ON TELLING

As notation is not given for the snow bunting's song, I have created a tune. You may use it
or make up your own. Papa Bunting would, of course, point to his chick's toes, wings,
eyes, and head as he sings. The parent should incorporate this if using the tale as a lap
story. Sometimes I point to toes, "wings," eyes, and heads of audience members during
the telling. The children will be glad to help you with the chick's crying, and for creative
dramatic re-enactments, add as many chicks as you need to the nest.

As Papa Bunting aggressively shoots arrows at Kutkha to retrieve his stolen song, this is not exactly a 'gentle' tale, but you can soften it by letting Papa Bunting shoot the small arrows "at" Kutkha's toes, rather than "into" them; maybe they bounce off, or Kutkha dodges. Your imagery will affect that of your audience. Despite Papa's violence against Kutkha, this tale seems gentle in tone to me. I particularly like the tender father image, as Papa Bunting creates a lullaby and sings his child to sleep.

Whose lit-tle toes are these?____

Whose lit-tle wings are these?____

Whose lit-tle eyes are these?____

Whose lit-tle head is this?____

COMPARATIVE NOTES

Variants of this tale appear in *Kutkha the Raven: Animal Stories of the North,* translated by Fainna Solasko (p. 5–10) and in *Life with Granny Kandiki* by Anna Garf (p. 13–16). These collections include Chuckchi, Nentsi, and Eskimo tales; they do not identify this tale by culture. Kenneth M. T. Jackson (Grey Eagle) has retold the tale in his *Let Us Honor That Rascal Raven.* Jackson took his tale from *Folke Eventyr Fra Sidir,* apparently the Norwegian translation of *Kutkha the Raven* mentioned above. Jackson's version uses sparrows as the nesting birds, and translates the lullaby as follows:

"Who is it that has such a cute little nose?
Who is it that has such dainty little toes?
Who is it that has such bright little eyes?
Who is it that now never cries?"

For another tale of song theft, see "Coyote's Crying Song" in *Twenty Tellable Tales* by Margaret Read MacDonald (p. 10–19). You will find extensive notes citing Pueblo, Zuñi, and Hopi variants there. My *Storyteller's Sourcebook* lists variants under G555.1.1 *Sing or I'll eat you. Ogre threatens.* "Kutkha" also incorporates Motif D1962.4.2 *Song used to lull children to sleep.*

LOOK BACK AND SEE

Teller: I went and I saw.
Audience: See so that WE may see.
Teller: I saw . . . I saw . . .

I saw a village where there had never been a dawn.
The village lay in darkness . . . all the time.

Just over the mountain lived a chief who OWNED the dawn.
He had a whole box full of dawn.
This chief was called . . . Lugeye.

The chief of the village of darkness decided to send a messenger
across the mountains to see if he could buy some dawn.

> "Here. Messenger.
> I give you one thousand cowries.
> Take these to Lugeye.
> Ask him to sell you some dawn."

The messenger took the cowries.
He began to climb the mountain.

"Eh . . . eh . . . eh . . . eh . . ."
He climbed the mountain.
"Eh . . . eh . . . eh . . . eh . . ."
He climbed the mountain.
"Eh . . . eh . . . eh . . ."
He went over the mountain.
"Eh . . . eh . . . eh . . ."
He went down the mountain.

He came to the village and he stopped.

> "Chief!
> Lugeye!
> I would like to buy some dawn.
> I have one thousand cowries.
> Will you sell?"

> "One thousand cowries!
> Of course I will sell.
> I have a whole BOX full of dawn.

Here.
Take some dawn.
Hold it tight.

"And remember
when you climb the mountain . . .
Don't . . . look . . . back."

"I'll remember."

"Eh . . . eh . . . eh . . . eh . . ."
He climbed the mountain. . . .

A Little Maid
sat by the gate of the village.
As he climbed, she opened her eyes
and watched him go.
Then she began to sing.

"Man . . .
Man . . .
You've taken the dawn of Lugeye.
Look back and see what Lugeye does.

"He sings with his arms!
He sings with his feet!
He wears beads like DANCING MAIDENS!

"They go che-ku
They go WA.
They go che-ku
They go WA."

The man STOPPED.
He TURNED.
He LOOKED.

SNAP!
CLAP!

The dawn was gone.

"Eh . . . eh . . . eh . . ."
He went down the mountain.
"Eh . . . eh . . . eh . . ."
He came off the mountain.

He came to his village and he stopped.

"Chief.
I had the dawn.
But I looked back
and I dropped it."

"Is there anyone here who can go and bring me the dawn?
Who is stronger?
You.
You go.
Here are two thousand cowries.
Go.
Bring me back the dawn."

"Eh . . . eh . . . eh . . . eh . . . "
He climbed the mountain.
"Eh . . . eh . . . eh . . . eh . . . "

14

He climbed the mountain.
"Eh . . . eh . . . eh . . ."
He went over the mountain.
"Eh . . . eh . . . eh . . ."
He came down the mountain.

He came to the village and he stopped.

>"Chief!
>Lugeye!
>I would like to buy some dawn.
>I have two thousand cowries.
>Will you sell?"

>"Two thousand cowries!
>Of course I'll sell.
>I have a whole BOX full of dawn.

>"Here.
>Take some dawn.
>But remember
>when you climb the mountain
>Don't . . . look . . . back."

>"I'll remember."

"Eh . . . eh . . . eh . . . eh . . ."
He climbed the mountain.

The Little Maid
at the gate of the village
opened her eyes and watched him go.

15

Then she began to sing.

> "Man . . .
> Man . . .
> You've taken the dawn of Lugeye.
> Look back and see what Lugeye does.

> "He sings with his arms!
> He sings with his legs!
> He wears beads like DANCING MAIDENS!

> "They go che-ku
> They go WA.

> They go che-ku
> They go WA."

He STOPPED.
He TURNED.
He LOOKED.

> SNAP!
> CLAP!

The dawn was gone.

"Eh . . . eh . . . eh . . ."
He went down the mountain.
"Eh . . . eh . . . eh . . ."
He came off the mountain.

He came to his village and he stopped.

"Chief.
I had the dawn.
But I looked back.
I dropped it."

"Isn't there ANYONE here who can bring that dawn to me?
Who among you is STRONGER?"

"I'll GO!
I'll GO!"
A little DOG spoke up.
"Please.
Let me go?"

"You?
You're only a . . . DOG."

"I know.
But I can do it.
Let me go?"

"You can TRY.
Here.
Take three thousand cowries.
Bring back some DAWN."

"Eh . . . eh . . . eh . . . eh . . ."
He climbed the mountain.

"Eh . . . eh . . . eh . . . eh . . ."
He climbed the mountain.
"Eh . . . eh . . . eh . . ."
He went over the mountain.
"Eh . . . eh . . . eh . . ."
He came down the mountain.

He came to the village and he stopped.

"Chief!
Lugeye!
I would like to buy some DAWN!"

"Dawn?
You?
You're only a little DOG."

"I know.
But I have three thousand cowries.
Please.
Could I buy some dawn?"

"Three thousand cowries?
Of course you can buy some dawn.
I have a whole BOX full of dawn.
Here.
Take some dawn.
Hold it tight in your teeth, little dog.

"And remember
When you climb the mountain
Don't . . . look . . . back."

18

The little dog held the dawn tight between his teeth.

"Mnn . . . mnn . . . mnn . . . mnn . . ."
He climbed the mountain.
"Mnn . . . mnn . . . mnn . . . mnn . . ."
He climbed the mountain.

The Little Maid
at the gate of the village
opened her eyes
and watched him go.
Then she began to sing.

     "Dog . . .
     Good dog. . . .
     You've taken the dawn of Lugeye.
     Look back and see what Lugeye does.

     "He sings with his arms!
     He sings with his legs!
     He wears beads like DANCING MAIDENS!

     "They go che-ku
     They go WA.
     They go che-ku
     They go WA."

"Mnn . . . mnn . . . mnn . . . mnn . . ."
He climbed the mountain.
"Mnn . . . mnn . . . mnn . . . mnn . . ."
He didn't look back.

"Good dog . . .
Good dog . . .
You've taken the dawn of Lugeye.
Look back and see what Lugeye does!

"He sings with his arms!
He sings with his legs!
He wears beads like DANCING MAIDENS!

They go che-ku
They go WA.
They go che-ku
They go WA."

"Mnn . . . mnn . . . mnn . . . mnn . . ."
He climbed the mountain.
"Mnn . . . mnn . . . mnn . . . mnn . . ."
He didn't look back.

"Mnn . . . mnn . . . mnn . . ."
He went over the mountain.
"Mnn . . . mnn . . . mnn . . . mnn . . ."
He didn't look back.

"Mnn . . . mnn . . . mnn . . ."
He came down the mountain.
"Mnn . . . mnn . . . mnn . . . mnn . . ."
He never looked back.

He came to his village and he stopped.

The little dog
opened his mouth.
The dawn came out.

It spread over the hills.
It covered the valley.
In this place where there had never been light . . .
there was DAWN.

When I saw that dawn
covering that valley,
it was so beautiful . . .
so beautiful . . .
I thought
I must go and tell my people what I have seen!

I saw . . . I saw . . .
THAT is what I saw.

NOTES ON TELLING

Before you begin telling this story, explain to your audience that they must reply in traditional Tanzanian fashion to the teller's opener, "I went and I saw . . . ," responding "See so that WE may see." You may want to explore the introduction to Peter Seitel's *See So That We May See: Performances and Interpretations of Traditional Tales from Tanzania* for a better understanding of Tanzanian tale-telling events.

This tale requires a lively, playful rendition. I slap my legs lightly in rhythm as the messengers climb the mountain. Speak the words in rhythm too, ending the rhythmical passage with: "He came to the village and he stopped." When the little dog volunteers, I make him pant a lot: "pant . . . pant . . . pant . . . pant . . . I'll go! . . . pant . . . pant . . . pant. . . ." As he climbs the hill, his teeth are tightly clenched, and so are yours. "Mnn . . . mnn . . . mnn . . . mnn . . ." Make a deep-throated grunting noise for him as he climbs.

The Little Maid by the gate is magical. She looks up and "opens her eyes" to watch him go, then begins to sing. Since no music is included in Seitel's book, I imagined a song. The music is given here, or you can imagine your own melody.

I encourage the audience to "dance with their arms, dance with their legs" along with me as we see Lugeye in action. It seems to me that the cowrie shells were probably on a string and that he is holding or wearing these, in addition to his other beads, as he dances. Seitel doesn't indicate this, but I envision the cowries strung into bead necklaces. How else could the little dog carry them?

Good dog, good dog. You've
tak - en the dawn of Lu - ge - ye.
Look back and see what Lu - ge - ye does.
He sings with his arms. He sings with his legs.—
He wears beads like danc - ing mai - dens.

I like to pretend I am asking the audience for volunteers to go for the dawn. Then I point to one and say "You can go." Everyone waves frantically to be the one chosen the third time, so I pick the most frantic waver and say, "A little DOG spoke up." This mock insult always delights the "dog."

Have fun with this one. Of course the children will want to act it out as soon as they have heard it.

COMPARATIVE NOTES

This story is loosely adapted from "Look Back and See What Lugeye Does!" in Peter Seitel's *See So That We May See: Performances and Interpretations of Traditional Tales from Tanzania* (p. 265–271). Seitel recorded the story from teller Ma Kelezensia Kahamba. You may want to consult that version for added touches for your own telling. Interesting elements that I chose not to use in my tellings are: the passing of certain Tanzanian villages on the road home (Lukindo, Kyema, etc.), a note at the end explaining that this is why you always see a dog at the chief's palace, and an intriguing image in which the chief finally sees the dawn approaching—"like when you see an automobile coming towards you in the darkness."

Several stories appear in *Trésors de la Tradition Orale Sakata: Proverbes, Mythes, Légends, Fables, Chansons et Divinettes de Sakata* by Lisa Colldén in which a village has never had fire. The chief sends a messenger to a neighboring village to acquire fire; tests ensue. The Sakata of Zaire also tell tales of wise, talking dogs who assist their owners. An interesting variant, "The Kingdom Without a Day," appears in *The Singing Turtle and Other Tales from Haiti* by Philippe Thoby-Marcelin and Pierre Marcelin. In this variant the hero sings to release dawn from the box, while the king sings for dawn not to break. A turtledove's droppings land on the king's nose, causing him to break his song, and the hero succeeds in singing dawn out of the box.

The notion of the sun being hoarded by one individual appears in many cultures. For example: Stith Thompson Motif A721 *Sun kept in box* (Siberian); A721.0.1 *Sun and moon kept in pots when they do not shine* (South American Indian, Native American); A721.0.2 *Sun shut up in pit* (India); A721.0.3 *Sun kept in case* (Jewish); A721.1 *Theft of sun* (Kaffir, Finnish, German, Eskimo, California Indian, Cashinawa); and also A725 *Man controls rising and setting of sun* (Irish, Jewish).

Kenneth Clarke's *A Motif-Index of the Folktales of Culture Area V West Africa* (Ph.D. diss., Indiana University, 1958) cites as A721.1 a Nigerian tale in which lizard retrieves the hoarded sun from cock, and a tale from Togo in which a wonder child holds the sun prisoner for three days.

KANJI-JO, THE NESTLINGS

On the banks of the Kanji River
a mother bird laid five eggs.
For a long time she sat on those eggs.
She fluffed her feathers over them and kept them warm.

Now and then she would sing to the eggs.
>"I laid five eggs long ago . . .
>By the Kanji River-o . . .
>I laid five eggs long ago. . . ."

Then she would stand and fluff her feathers.
>"Kanji-jo, gebeti-jo.
>Kanji-jo, gebeti-jo.
>Kanji-jo, gebeti-jo."

Just when the chicks were about to pop from their eggs
a hunter came by.
He threw a net over the mother bird and carried her off.
After a while, she managed to escape,
but by that time she was far from her nest.

Meanwhile, the sun shone so warmly on the eggs
that they began to hatch.
The first egg rolled over.
    "peck . . . peck . . . peck . . ."
Out came a baby bird.

The second egg began to move.
    "peck . . . peck . . . peck . . ."
Out popped another.

The third egg . . .
    "peck . . . peck . . . peck . . ."

The fourth egg . . .
    "peck . . . peck . . . peck . . ."

The fifth egg . . .
    "peck . . . peck . . . peck . . .
    peck . . . peck . . . peck . . .
    peck . . . peck . . . PECK!"

There were five baby birds in the nest.

    "Ma-má! Ma-má! Ma-má!"
They began at once to cry for their mother.

"Ma-má! Ma-má! Ma-má!"
But there was no mother there for the chicks.

"Our mother has gone!
We must look for our mother!"

The little birds climbed down out of their nest.
They began wobbling down the road on their weak little legs.

"Ma-má! Ma-má! Ma-má!"

They met Mrs. Bushfowl.
"Ma-má! Ma-má! Ma-má!"
"Oh dear, are these MY children?" said Mrs. Bushfowl.
"I didn't know I had five children.
But they are calling me 'Ma-má'.
They must be mine."
She took the little chicks into her nest.
She fed them their supper.
She put them to bed for the night.

In the morning the five little birds looked at their new mother.
She was big and brown and fluffy.
They were small and their feathers seemed to be blue.

"Pardon us, but are you really our mother?
Our mother sang a beautiful song when we were in our eggs.
Would you sing your song, so we will know you are our
mother?"

Mrs. Bushfowl fluffed up her feathers.
She began to sing.

"ko-ko-ye! ko-ko-ye! ko-ko-ye!
ko-ko-ye! ko-ko-ye! ko-ko-ye!"

"THAT'S not our mother's song.
Our mother sang a beautiful song.
She sang like this:

"I laid five eggs long ago . . .
By the Kanji River-o . . .
I laid five eggs long ago. . . .

"Kanji-jo, gebeti-jo.
Kanji-jo, gebeti-jo.
Kanji-jo, gebeti-jo."

"That's a lovely song," said Mrs. Bushfowl.
"But I can't sing like that.
I must not be your mother.
You'd better go look for her."

So the little birds went on down the road.
They were feeling stronger now.
They marched along calling:

"Ma-má! Ma-má! Ma-má!"

In the evening they met Mrs. Dove.
"Ma-má! Ma-má! Ma-má!"

"Oh my, are these MY children?" said Mrs. Dove.
"I didn't know I had five children.
But they are calling me 'Ma-má!'
They must be mine."

She took them into her nest.
She fed them their supper.
She put them to bed for the night.

In the morning the five little chicks looked at their new mother.
She was shaped in a special dove way.
She seemed not like them at all.

"Pardon us, but are you really our mother?
Our mother sang a beautiful song when we were in our eggs.
Would you sing your song, so we will know you are our
mother?"

Mrs. Dove stretched out her graceful neck and began to sing.

"coo . . . ooooo
coo . . . ooooo
coo . . . ooooo."

"THAT'S not our mother's song.
She sang a beautiful song.
She sang like this:

"I laid five eggs long ago . . .
By the Kanji River-o . . .
I laid five eggs long ago. . . .

28

"Kanji-jo, gebeti-jo.
Kanji-jo, gebeti-jo.
Kanji-jo, gebeti-jo."

"That IS a lovely song," said Mrs. Dove.
I can't sing like that.
I am certainly not your mother.
You must go and look for her."

So off went the little birds.
"Ma-má! Ma-má! Ma-má!"

That evening they met Mrs. Hummingbird.

"Ma-má! Ma-má! Ma-má!"
"Oh my, these children are calling me 'Ma-má!'
I didn't know I had five children.
But they must be mine.
Well, come into my nest and I'll give you your dinner."

Mrs. Hummingbird put the five baby birds into her tiny nest.
It was so small they had to squeeze to fit.
She gave them their supper.
She put them to bed.

In the morning the five little birds looked at their new mother.
She was very tiny.
She was smaller than any of THEM.

"Can this really be our mother?
"Our mother sang a beautiful song when we were in our eggs.

29

Could you sing your song, so we will know that you are really
our mother?"

Mrs. Hummingbird flew up and began to buzz around the nest making
her song:

"Kawunggg . . .
Kawunggg . . .
Kawunggg . . ."

"THAT'S not our mother's song.
Our mother sang a beautiful song.

She sang like this:
"I laid five eggs long ago . . .
By the Kanji River-o . . .
I laid five eggs long ago . . .

Kanji-jo, gebeti-jo.
Kanji-jo, gebeti-jo.
Kanji-jo, gebeti-jo."

"What a lovely song!
I can't sing like that.
I am not your mother.

"But you are such lovely little birds
and you sing such a fine song
I would like to give you a present before you go."

Mrs. Hummingbird gave each of them a little present.

> "Here is one for you . . . and you . . . and you . . . and
> you . . . and you.
> I hope you find your mother."

The little birds went on their way.

> "Ma-má! Ma-má! Ma-má!"

Meanwhile, the mother had escaped from the hunter.
She flew back to her home, looking for her chicks.
But the nest was empty.

She flew down the road.

> "Mrs. Bushfowl! Have you seen my children?"
> "Were there five of them?"
> "Yes."
> "Did they sing a lovely song?"
> "I expect they did."
> "They went down the road just two days ago."

The mother bird flew down the road.

> "Mrs. Dove! Have you seen my children?"
> "Were there five of them?"
> "Yes."
> "Were they singing a beautiful song?"
> "I expect they were."
> "They went down this road, just yesterday."

The mother bird flew down the road.

> "Mrs. Hummingbird! Have you seen my children?"

"Were there five of them?"

"Yes."

"Did they have blue feathers like yours?"

"I believe they should have."

"Were they singing a fine song?"

"I believe they were."

"Then they were just here.

They went down this road."

"Aaaahhhhh. . . . . . ."

The mother bird ran after her children.

"Chick . . . chick . . . chick . . . chick . . ."

"Ma-má! Ma-má! Ma-má!"

Then the chicks heard her.

They turned and looked at their mother.

Her feathers were blue like theirs, only more brilliant.

She was shaped just like they were, only bigger.

She was just the right size to be their mother.

The five little chicks RAN to their mother.

     "MA-MÁ! MA-MÁ! MA-MÁ! MA-MÁ! MA-MÁ!"

     "CHICK! CHICK! CHICK! CHICK! CHICK!"

They hugged one another.

They ruffled one another's feathers.

The mother bird made a nest for her babies.

She fed them.

She put them to bed for the night.

     "Sing us your song!

     Sing us your song!

     So we will know you are really our mother!"

"Wait," said the mother bird.

"In the morning we will sing.

In the morning we will dance.

In the morning I will teach you how to fly."

In the morning the mother bird woke up first of all.

She stretched her head way over the nest and looked at her sleeping children.

And she began to sing.

"I laid five eggs long ago . . .

By the Kanji River-o . . .

I laid five eggs long ago. . . ."

When the little birds heard that

they jumped to their feet and began to flap their wings and dance!

"Kanji-jo, gebeti-jo!

Kanji-jo, gebeti-jo!

Kanji-jo, gebeti-jo!"

It really was their mother.

And all day long they danced in that nest.

"Kanji-jo, gebeti-jo . . .

Kanji-jo, gebeti-jo . . .

Kanji-jo, gebeti-jo. . . ."

NOTES ON TELLING

The mother's song is sweet and plaintive, but when the Kanji-jo chorus begins, the baby birds should roust about, flapping their wings in the beginnings of a dance. At the tale's end, they should really cut loose as they dance in the nest. The Mende text states, "That day there was a big dance in that nest; liquor flowed freely." It ends "Of course, these little creatures brought riches into the world. What I have explained is what happened at one time."

Though it is not in the Mende text at all, sometimes I add the following tag ending to the story:

> And then the mother taught them how to fly.
> They spread their little wings
> and soared through the sky.
> All day long they flew.
> And as they flew, they sang,
>
> > "Kanji-jooooohhhh. . . .
> > Gebeti-jooooohhhh . . .
> > Kanji-jooooohhhh . . .
> > Gebeti-jooooohhhh . . ."

This is performed with outspread arms as the birds soar.

The tendency for folktales to recreate themselves is amazing. As I began telling the tale, I found I wanted to see the birds swooping and singing as the tale ended. So I added this bit to my telling. Because it was my own addition, I considered it not authentic and left it out of the version I prepared for this collection. Then, while working on the tale notes for this book I discovered a second Mende variant in which the teller describes the birds' swooping and singing in an ending almost identical to mine!

The creative dramatic possibilities for this story are obvious—lots of parts, lots of dance, easy songs.

As no music was included in the source, I have created a tune for the chicks' song. Use it, if you like, or create your own.

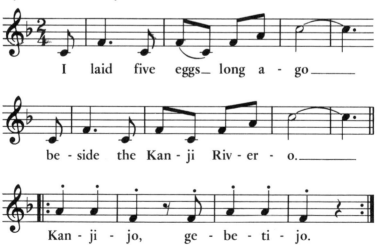

I laid five eggs— long a - go____
be - side the Kan - ji Riv - er - o.____
Kan - ji - jo, ge - be - ti - jo.

34

COMPARATIVE NOTES

This is based on a story in *Royal Antelope and Spider: West African Mende Tales* by Marion Kilson (Cambridge, Mass.: Press of the Langdon Associates, 1976), p. 128–135. The entire Mende text is given, as well as an English translation. The tale was "recorded by a man from Bumpe in Bo on April 16, 1960."

I have altered the birds' chant to make it easier for children to repeat. The original translation is:

> Our mother bore us long ago . . .
> Our mother bore us long ago . . .
> Our mother bore us on the Kanji.
> The Kanji River sat on the eggs.
> The eggs became smooth.
> And the eggs have hatched.
> Kanji-jo, gbeti-jo
> Kanji-jo, gbeti-jo
> Kanji-jo, gbeti-jo.

The Mende text is

> Mu nje mu lea wo
> Mu nje mu lea wo
> Mu nje mu leilo Kanji-ma-o
> Kanji pienga i lenga ngawu ma
> Ngawui na tetea
> Kanji-jo, gbeti-jo
> Kanji-jo, gbeti-jo
> Kanji-jo, gbeti-jo

Though the chant says that the river sat on the eggs, the story says, "she had put the eggs in a high tree, the river did not touch them. The birds stayed in the nest until they were able to eat the earth, they pecked at the earth. God continued to feed the little birds; their feathers began to come out and they were able to shout."

The birds used in the original tale are crow, bushfowl, woodcock, and hummingbird. The nestlings are not identified by species.

35

It may be interesting to contrast the sweetness of this tale with two West African tales of nestlings. *Animals Mourn For Da Leopard and Other West African Tales* by Peter Dorliae (p. 56–62) includes a Mano tale of Liberia in which a Guinea Hen asks each egg what it will do for her when hatched. In this tale a sixth egg replies, "Nothing", so she abandons him, but he follows her, acting insufferably to everyone he meets, (MacDonald's *Storyteller's Sourcebook* J267.1.1). In *Fourteen Hundred Cowries and Other African Tales* by Abayomi Fuja (p. 116–119), a Yoruba tale tells of the ega parents who tear up their nests and leave to be rid of their obnoxious nestlings. The chicks follow them nevertheless, (MacDonald A2431.3.15). Stith Thompson's *Motif-Index of Folk-Literature* cites another version, from India, J646.2 *Bird hears voices from within unhatched eggs and flies away: voices plot to dine on their bird-mother when they are born.* In the Mende text from which "Kanji-jo" was taken, the mother bird just flies away from the nest without reason. So, to make sense of her leaving for my audiences, I invented the hunter. When you remove the hunter, the tale seems similar to the three "bratty chick" stories above, except in its denouement.

Three variants of this tale are given in full in *Defiant Maids and Stubborn Farmers: Tradition and Invention in Mende Story Performance* by Donald Cosentino (Cambridge: Cambridge University Press, 1982), p. 55–66. In these variants the teller trains the audience to sing a refrain to the baby chicks' chorus. In one variant the mother bird goes off when she hears them coming, but in the other two variants they are reunited. In the most fully developed telling the mother and her chicks glide in the sky and sing their song to celebrate: "So the merriment was so great nothing could stop it. These birds swooped in the sky: you see them going bengu-bengu-bengu. It's that dance that they're dancing."

DOMINGO SIETE

Once there were two brothers who lived together.

The older brother treated the younger brother very poorly.
He bossed him around constantly
and cuffed him when he did not obey.
He ran the poor boy ragged with errands and work
and fed him almost nothing.

One day, when the younger brother was sent to cut wood in the
    mountains, he decided to run away.
Higher and higher into the mountain range he wandered.
He had nothing to eat but the fruit of the cactus plants.
On ulúa and ucle fruit he would survive.

When he reached the very peak of the mountain ridge,
he climbed a hugh algarroba tree to shelter for the night.
But in the middle of the night he was awakened by a horrible noise!
Looking down, he saw that the tree was surrounded by wild-looking
    brujos!
Holding hands, they were dancing around the algarroba tree
    and singing:

> "Lunes, Martes, Miércoles tres.
> Jueves, Viernes, . . ."

But there their song stopped.
They could not find a way to end it.

> "Lunes, Martes Miércoles tres.
> Jueves, Viernes, . . ."

They were looking for a rhyme.
But they could not figure it out.

> "Lunes, Martes, Miércoles tres.
> Jueves, Viernes, . . ."

It was FRUSTRATING!

The brujos began to argue among themselves.
No one knew how to end the song.
Soon they were punching each other in a terrible fight,
arguing over the song's ending.

When they had worn themselves out
   they got up and tried the song again.

      "Lunes, Martes, Miércoles tres.
      Jueves, Viernes, . . ."

Watching from his tree, the boy felt sorry for the poor brujos.
Everyone knows that the days of the week are:

      Lunes, Martes, Miércoles
      Monday, Tuesday, Wednesday

      Jueves, Viernes, SÁBADO
      Thursday, Friday, SATURDAY

And everyone knows how to count:
      Uno, Dos, TRES
      One, Two, THREE

      Quatro, Cinco, SEIS
      Four, Five, SIX.

So when the brujos started again:
      "Lunes, Martes, Miércoles tres.
      Jueves, Viernes, . . ."
The boy called down to them . . .
      "Sábado SEIS!

That was it!

The brujos began to turn somersaults with delight!
They danced and sang!
>"Lunes, Martes, Miércoles tres.
>Jueves, Viernes, Sábado SEIS!
>"Lunes, Martes, Miércoles tres.
>Jueves, Viernes, Sábado SEIS!"

They were so delighted to have their rhyme completed,
they pulled the boy from the tree
and began to pile presents before him.
>Flour, cheese, honey they brought.
>And then . . . two burros loaded with coins!

With these presents, the boy returned home.
The older brother was pleased enough to see him
>when he came bearing such gifts.
He treated him quite well for a while.
But after a few weeks, the flour, cheese, and honey had been eaten.
And the coins were soon spent.

>"The coins are all gone.
>Take me back where you got them
>so we can get MORE."

But the younger brother had been warned not to bring anyone to the
>mountain.
He would not go.

"Then if YOU won't go for the coins.
Tell me the way and *I* will go," ordered the older brother.

And the younger brother, for fear of getting another beating,
told how to find the algarroba tree on the mountain top.

The next Saturday the older brother set off,
He carried his long knife at his side
and strode along singing boldly:

> "I'm from the barrio of Bracho
> where it RAINS but never lightly.
> I am not afraid of bullies.
> No brujo will meddle with me."

He reached the algarroba tree just before midnight and climbed into the
tree's lower branches.

Exactly at midnight the brujos arrived.
They began at once to sing and dance, circling the tree.
> "Lunes, Martes, Miércoles tres.
> Jueves, Viernes, Sábado SEIS!"

> "Lunes, Martes, Miércoles tres.
> Jueves, Viernes, Sábado SEIS!"
> "Here is where I get my prize!" thought the elder brother.
> "I can add to THAT rhyme.
> Everyone knows that 'Domingo', Sunday, is the SEVENTH
>   day of the week
>   . . . that's 'Siete'."
He did not stop to think whether this would fit the rhyme.

"Lunes, Martes, Miércoles tres.
Jueves, Viernes, Sábado SEIS!"

And the foolish brother shouted out:
"Domingo SIETE!"

The beat was broken.
The dance stopped.
"Domingo SIETE?
Domingo SIETE?
Get out of here with your 'Domingo SIETE!' "
The brujos were furious.
Their lovely rhyme was spoiled.
Their dance was ruined.

They pulled that brother down from the tree
and beat him to a pulp.
When he came to the next morning, it was all he could do to drag
    himself down the mountain and back home.
The younger brother took pity on him and nursed him back to health.
And was he cured of his overbearing ways?
Well, to a certain extent.
From then on, whenever the older brother began acting bossy, the
    younger brother need simply say, "Domingo SIETE,"
and the older brother would remember his manners.

Ever since then, when someone forgets to think and utters some
    stupidity,
folks turn and jeer:
"Get out of here with your 'Domingo SIETE!' "

42

NOTES ON TELLING

It works well to use a drum with the song. This emphasizes the frustration of the broken rhythm. The rhythm I use is given here.

This story is told widely throughout the world, and often the dancing creatures are dwarfs. I use the Castellano word "brujo" rather than the English translation "witch" in my version. If the use of "witch" tales is a problem with your audiences, you might have to turn them back into dwarfs. However, since Berta Bautista, a friend from Jujuy, an Andean province of Argentina, told me many tales of witches in those mountains, but never mentioned a dwarf, I am keeping the "brujos" myself. The tale mentions that they are both male and female, and scantily clad.

I suggest that you talk about the Spanish names for the days of the week and the Spanish numbers from one to seven, before you begin the story. This tale seems to work best with the Spanish rhyme, though there are English-language variants in use.

For example, you could use:

> Monday, Tuesday, three is Wednesday.
> Thursday, Friday, six is Saturday.
> Sunday is SEVEN!

COMPARATIVE NOTES

This tale is based on "Salir Con Su Domingo Siete" in *Juan Soldao: Cuentos Folklóricos De La Argentina*, compiled by Susana Chertudi (p. 137–140).

This is a variant of Motif F344.1 *Fairies remove hunchback's hump (or replace it)*.

My *Storyteller's Sourcebook* lists variants from Friesland, Germany (Grimms), Haiti, Ireland, Italy, Spain, and Wales. Fairies, dwarfs, or goblins may be the dancers. Usually, a hunchback has his hump removed as a reward for completing the song. A second hunchback tries and is given another hump. Or, the second man's efforts cause the first to have his hump replaced. Japanese, Chinese, and Korean variants tell of an old man with a wen on his cheek who has the wen removed, a second greedy old man tries to do the same and is given the first man's wen in addition to his own. The dancers are *tengu* in the Japanese variants.

Susana Chertudi notes finding a Costa Rican variant, which was very similar to the Argentinian tale with the exception of the specific Argentinian elements of the cactus fruit, and the *copla* which the elder brother sings in bravado. Only in the Argentinian version are the two main characters brothers.

For an especially well-developed Mexican variant see "The Hunchback" in *Tongues of the Monte* by J. Frank Dobie. This story is also reprinted in *World Tales for Creative Dramatics and Storytelling* by Burdette S. Fitzgerald (p. 245–251).

TURKEY GIRL

This is the story of a Zuñi girl.
She lived outside the village and cared for a flock of turkeys.

Every morning this girl would feed her turkeys.
Every noontime she would feed them and put out fresh water.
Every evening that girl was there to feed her turkeys
and provide their water.

She thought of them as her "Little Children."
They called her their "Little Mother."

One morning the girl heard a sound coming from the village.
It was the sound of drums.

"The Lapalehakya Dance!
They must be dancing the Lapalehakya!
Oh, I wish I could go to the dance.

"Turkeys . . . Little Children . . .
Do you think I could go to the dance today?"

The turkeys were much upset at that.
They shook their heads and muttered.

"Tot . . . tot . . . tot . . . tot . . . tot . . . tot . . . tot . . .
Who'd give us our water?

"Tot . . . tot . . . tot . . . tot . . . tot . . . tot . . . tot . . .
Who'd give us our food?

"Tot . . . tot . . . tot . . . tot . . . tot . . . tot . . . tot . . .
Who'd look after US?

"You're our Little Mother!"

"You are right," said the girl.
"I am responsible for you all.
I won't go to the dance."
And she said no more about it.

But the next day she heard the drums again.

"Oh, it is the SECOND day of the dance!
Turkeys . . . Little Children . . .
Do you think I could go to the dance today?"

46

The turkeys were very upset.

"Tot . . . tot . . . tot . . . tot . . . tot . . . tot . . . tot . . .
Who'd give us our water?

"Tot . . . tot . . . tot . . . tot . . . tot . . . tot . . . tot . . .
Who'd give us our food?

"Tot . . . tot . . . tot . . . tot . . . tot . . . tot . . . tot . . .
Who'd look after US?

"You're our Little Mother!"

"Of course you are right.
I should not go off to the dance.
I won't mention it again."

But that night she climbed onto the roof of her house.
She looked toward the village.
She could see the lights from the fires.
She could hear the singing.

"They are all dancing and singing," she thought.
"They are all dressed up and having a good time."

The next day the girl heard the drums again.

"It is the THIRD day of the dance!
The dance only lasts four days.
Oh, I wish that I could go.

"Turkeys . . . Little Children.
Maybe I could go to the dance today?"

"Tot . . . tot . . . tot . . . tot . . . tot . . . tot . . . tot . . .
Who'd give us our water?

"Tot . . . tot . . . tot . . . tot . . . tot . . . tot . . . tot . . .
Who'd give us our food?

"Tot . . . tot . . . tot . . . tot . . . tot . . . tot . . . tot . . .
Who'd look after US?

"You're our Little Mother!"

"I know you are right.
But I DO want to go.
Maybe tomorrow . . . ?"

That night the girl took yuca and made suds.
She washed all over her body.
Her skin felt clean and shining.
She washed her hair and braided it.

In the morning the girl called her turkeys to her.
    "I have decided.
    Today I am going to the dance.
    I will dance the Lapalehakya with the others.
    I promise I will come back in time to give you your food and
        water.

Then the turkey who was eldest of them all stepped forward.

48

"If you have decided,
then you will go.
But listen carefully to what I tell you.
Dance FOUR DANCES. No more.
Four dances. No more.
If you dance longer
things will be very bad for us."

"I promise.
I will dance just four dances.
I will come home to feed you."

"Turkeys gather round," said the Turkey Elder.
"Our girl is going to the dance.
She has decided.
Let's give her presents before she goes."

The turkeys gathered around the girl in a circle.
They began to sing their turkey song.
They began to make magic.

"Tot . . . tot . . . tot . . . tot . . . tot . . . tot . . . tot . . .
Hu-li! Hu-li! Hu-li! Hu-li!
Tot . . . tot . . . tot . . . tot . . . tot . . . tot . . . tot . . .
Hu-li! Hu-li! Hu-li! Hu-li!"

The first turkey stopped and raised its wings.
Out dropped a pair of beaded slippers!

"Oh, THANK you!" said the girl.
"I can DANCE in these!"
She put on the slippers.

"Tot . . . tot . . . tot . . . tot . . . tot . . . tot . . . tot . . .
Hu-li! Hu-li! Hu-li! Hu-li!"
The second turkey stopped and raised its wings.
Out fell a fancy dress!

"I can wear this to the DANCE!
THANK you."
The girl put on the dress.

The turkeys began to circle her again.
"Tot . . . tot . . . tot . . . tot . . . tot . . . tot . . . tot . . .
Hu-li! Hu-li! Hu-li! Hu-li!"
The third turkey raised its wings.
Out dropped a string of bright blue beads!

"Thank you! Thank you!"
The girl put on the beads.

"Tot . . . tot . . . tot . . . tot . . . tot . . . tot . . . tot . . .
Hu-li! Hu-li! Hu-li! Hu-li!"

The fourth turkey raised its wings.
Down fell ornaments for her hair!

The girl fixed the ornaments in her hair.
She turned round to show the turkeys.
She was beautiful.

"Remember . . . four dances. No more."

"Yes. Yes. I'll remember."

The girl was running off down the road toward the village.

When the people saw her coming,
they couldn't guess who she might be.
They had only seen her in ragged clothing before,
tending her turkeys.

"Who is that beautiful new girl?
Look at her dress.
Who can she be?"

"Come and DANCE with us!" they called.

The girl began to dance.
And she danced one dance.
And she had a good time.
And she danced two dances.
And she had a good time.
And she danced three dances.
And she had a good time.
And she danced four dances.
And she had a good time.
And she danced five dances.
And she had a good time.
And she danced six dances.
And she had a good time.
And she danced seven dances . . .

The turkeys were waiting.
The girl did not return to give them their food at noontime.

All through the long hot afternoon the turkeys stood without any water.
The girl did not return at sunset to give them their meal.

The Turkey Elder opened the gate of their pen.
"Our girl has forgotten us.
We will go back to the wild.
We will take care of ourselves."

The turkeys began slowly to walk away up the canyon.
"Tot . . . tot . . . tot . . . tot . . . tot . . . tot . . . tot . . .
Tot . . . tot . . . tot . . . tot . . . tot . . . tot . . . tot . . ."

The girl stopped dancing.
She knew that turkey language.
"My TURKEYS!"
The girl ran to her home.
It was too late.
The turkeys were disappearing up the canyon.
"Tot . . . tot . . . tot . . . tot . . . tot . . . tot . . . tot . . ."

"My turkeys, come back!
I'll never go away again.
I promise."

The turkeys did not even look back.
"Tot . . . tot . . . tot . . . tot . . . tot . . . tot . . . tot . . ."

When they came to the end of the canyon
they walked straight up the canyon walls to the mesa above.

If you go there today
you will find wild turkeys all over the mesas by the Zuñi mountains.
You can still see their tracks in the canyon
where they climbed away from their girl.
But they never returned to live again
in the valley by the village.

NOTES ON TELLING

I tend to waddle a bit when my turkeys "tot . . . tot . . . tot." They are really quite grumpy and petulant with their Little Mother. The rhythmic sequence at the dance, "And she danced one dance. . . ," is my own addition to the tale. You can easily omit it if it doesn't seem right for you. I wanted to show the passage of time at the dance. The audience members are counting too and they are shocked when she dances the fifth dance. The creative dramatic possibilities for this piece are obvious.

COMPARATIVE NOTES

This tale is usually perceived as a Cinderella variant, Motif R221 *Heroine's threefold flight from ball.* However in the Zuñi variant the girl's relationship with her turkeys seems more important than her grand time at the dance. Her overstaying at the ball results in the neglect of her charges.

A Zuñi variant is included in Virginia Haviland's *North American Legends* (p. 76). The tale also has Spanish variants and Harry Berson uses this motif in a European setting in his picture book *Turkey Girl.* In *Fantastic Theater: Puppets and Plays for Young Performers and Young Audiences* Judy Sierra adapts the tale as a puppet play, "The Turkey Maiden" (p. 204–211).

Elsie Clews Parsons includes a version of this tale as told by Tsatiselu of Zuñi in "Pueblo-Indian Folk-Tales of Spanish Provenience," *Journal of American Folk-Lore* 31, 120: (1918) 234–35. Tsatiselu's variant includes sisters with whom the turkey girl does not get along. She calls the turkeys her "younger sisters." They eat the lice from her hair to clean her up for the dance, then clap their wings and "down from the air fell" first a blanket dress (*yatone*), a belt (*ehina*), a hair belt (*tsutokehnina*), and moccasins (*mok-*

wawe). The turkeys braid her hair and put it up for her. The dance takes place at Matsaki and is called "lapalehakya" (parrots-tell). The turkeys flee to Kyakima, then to Tonae-teanawa (turkey tracks), where they drink at the spring, and finally to the spring at Shoya-k'oskwi, where one still finds many wild turkeys.

Frank Hamilton Cushing includes a lengthy version in his *Zuñi Folktales* (p. 54–64). His girl lives at Matsaki but goes to the Dance of the Sacred Bird at Old Zuñi. The turkeys ask her to remove her clothing item by item and tread on it to transform it into lovely raiment. They cough up jewelry to adorn her, and fan their wings, singing and dancing around the girl to clean her and make her beautiful. They flee to the Canyon of the Cottonwoods, behind Thunder Mountain, through the Gateway of Zuñi and up the valley. The rocks leading to Cañon Mesa (Shoya-k'oskwi) show their tracks and other figures, which represent the songs they sang, are graven on the rocks. The turkeys say of her, "Behold, this our maiden mother, though so humble and poor, deserves, forsooth, her hard life, because, were she more prosperous, she would be unto others as others now are unto her." Cushing concludes, "After all, the gods dispose of men according as men are fitted; and if the poor be poor in heart and spirit as well as in appearance, how will they be aught but poor to the end of their days?"

The Turkey's song, as given by Cushing, includes these lines:

> K'yaanaa, to! to!
> K'yaanaa, to! to!
> Ye ye!
>
> K'yaanaa, to! to!
> K'yaanaa, to! to!
> Yee huli huli!
>
> Ye ye huli huli
> Tot-tot, tot-tot, tot-tot
> Huli huli!

He translates this as "Up the river to! to!, Sing ye ye!"

LITTLE CRICKET'S MARRIAGE

A. Ms. Cricket Takes a Husband

Once there was a little cricket who wanted to get married.
She went to her mother and said "Momma, Momma! I want to get
married."
"Well, you must go find a husband," said her mother.
"Look carefully and choose someone who is just right for you."

Little Cricket went out and searched for a husband.
"tzee . . . tzee . . . tzee. . . ," she ran along.
She met Mr. Camel. She liked the way he looked.
"Ooohhh, Mr. Camel . . . Mr. Camel.
Do you want to marry me?"

The camel looked down at the tiny cricket.
     "Baaa. Baaa. Marry you?
     Why would I want to marry you?
     You're nothing but a little cricket.
     A cricket!"

This made the little cricket furious.
     "Cricket, cricket yourself!
     Who do you think you are?"

Well, the camel was impressed by her attitude.
     "What a spunky little cricket!
     Maybe I will marry you after all."

     "Then . . .
     Put your money in my sleeve
     and I'll go ask my momma," said Little Cricket.

The little cricket ran home to her mother.
     "Tzee . . . tzee . . . tzee . . .
     Momma! Momma! I have a suitor!
     He wants to marry me."

     "Well what is his name?"
     "His name is Mr. Camel."

     "That's a nice name.
     What does he look like?"

     "I like the way he looks.
     His eyes are very big.
     His ears are very big.

His nose is very big.
He's BIG ALL OVER!"

"NO, NO, Little Cricket.
You cannot marry Mr. Camel.
He is TOO BIG for you.
He might step on you and squash you.
Find another suitor."

"Ooohhh. That's too bad . . ."

Little Cricket ran back to Mr. Camel.
"Tzee . . . tzee . . . tzee . . .
Mr. Camel, I'm sorry.
I can't marry you.
You're TOO BIG!"

Little Cricket went looking for another suitor.
"Tzee . . . tzee . . . tzee . . ."
She met Mr. Bull. She liked the way he looked.
"Mr. Bull . . . Mr. Bull . . .
Do you want to marry me?"

The Bull looked down at her.
"Blaaa. Blaaa. Marry you?
Why would I want to marry you?
You're nothing but a little cricket.
A cricket!"

The little cricket was furious.
"Cricket, cricket yourself!
Who do you think you are?"

57

The bull was impressed by her attitude.
"What a spunky little cricket!
Maybe I will marry you after all."

"Then . . .
Put your money in my sleeve
and I'll go ask my momma."

The little cricket ran back to her mother.
"Tzee . . . tzee . . . tzee . . .
Momma! Momma! I have a suitor.
He wants to marry me."

"Well, what is his name?"
"His name is Mr. Bull."

"That's a nice name.
What does he look like?"

"I like the way he looks.
His eyes are very big.
His ears are very big.
His nose is very big.
He's BIG ALL OVER!"

"NO, NO, Little Cricket!
You cannot marry Mr. Bull.
He is TOO BIG for you.
He might roll over on you and squash you.
Find another suitor."

"Ooohhh. That's too bad . . ."

Little Cricket went back to Mr. Bull.
"Tzee . . . tzee . . . tzee. . .
Mr. Bull, I'm sorry.
I can't marry you.
You're TOO BIG!"

She went on down the road looking for a suitor.
"Tzee . . . tzee . . . tzee . . ."
Little Cricket met Mr. Mouse.
"Mr. Mouse . . . Mr. Mouse . . .
Do you want to marry me?"

Mr. Mouse looked at the little cricket.
"Tzee. Tzee. Marry you?
Why would I want to marry you?
You're nothing but a little cricket.
A cricket!"

The little cricket was furious.
"Cricket, cricket yourself!
Who do you think you are?"

The mouse was impressed by her attitude.
"What a spunky little cricket!
Maybe I will marry you after all."

"Then . . .
Put your money in my sleeve
And I'll go ask my momma."

The little cricket ran back to her mother.
                    "Tzee . . . tzee . . . tzee . . .
                    Momma! Momma! I have another suitor!
                    He wants to marry me."

                    "Well, what is his name?"
                    "His name is Mr. Mouse."

                    "That's a nice name.
                    What does he look like?"

                    "I like the way he looks.
                    His eyes are very tiny.
                    His ears are very tiny.
                    His nose is very tiny.
                    He's TINY ALL OVER!"

                    "Little Cricket, that is the husband for you!
                    He is just your size.
                    Marry him at once!"

So Little Cricket ran back to Mr. Mouse.
                    "Tzee . . . tzee . . . tzee . . .
                    Mr. Mouse! Mr. Mouse!
                    Momma says we can get married!"

And so they were married.

That is the end of the first part of the story.
Are you ready for the second half? Here it comes.

B. Ms. Cricket Does Her Laundry

Little Cricket and Mr. Mouse were married for a week.

And at the end of the week

they had accumulated a whole pile of dirty laundry!

Well, that's the real world.

First you get married

and then you start the housework.

Mr. Mouse and Little Cricket decided to take a day off and go do their laundry.

They went looking for a good spot to wash.

Mr. Mouse ran in front, "tzee . . . tzee . . . tzee . . ."

Little Cricket ran behind, "tzee . . . tzee . . . tzee. . . "

They came to the Sea of Acre (the Mediterranean Sea).

The waves seemed very high to the two.

Mr. Mouse looked all around.

> "This will never do.
> We have to wash all of our dirty laundry
> and take baths besides.
> There's not enough water here."

So they turned around and went to the Sea of Tiberius (the Sea of
Galilee).

The waves still seemed very high.

Mr. Mouse looked all around.

> "This will never do.
> We have to wash all of our dirty laundry
> and take baths besides.
> There's not enough water here."

So they turned and went back inland.

The little cricket began to call

> "Husband! Husband!
> I have found just the spot for us!"

Mr. Mouse hurried over.

Little Cricket had found the hoofprint of a donkey.

It was sunk into the mud and had filled with rainwater.

> "It's perfect!" said Mr. Mouse.
> "There is plenty of water to wash our laundry
> and for each of us to take a bath too.
> I'll go to town and buy the soap."

And Mr. Mouse ran off to town.

While he was gone Little Cricket sat down on the edge of the hoofprint
full of water.

She dangled her toes in the water.

Then she thought,
> "I believe I will go ahead and take my bath before my
> husband comes back."

She jumped into the hole and began to wash herself all over.
But when she had finished her bath
she found she could not climb out again.
The sides were too steep
The hoofprint was too deep.
She was trapped at the bottom.
"Help help! Help help!"

Just then a man rode by on his horse.
She heard the bells jingling on his bridle and began to call.
> "O Uncle, up on your horse
> jingling your bell,
> say to the mouse:
> 'The Lady of the House
> into the water fell!' "

The horseman listened.
> "I thought I heard a voice."

She called again
> "O Uncle, up on your horse
> jingling your bell,
> say to the mouse:
> 'The Lady of the House
> into the water fell!' "

The horseman leaned over and looked into the donkey's hoofprint.

There he saw the little cricket struggling in the water and calling.
The horseman laughed and rode on.

The little cricket folded her arms and glared after him.
  "And if you don't do it,
  may your bottom get stuck to your horse!"

The man rode on into town and reached his house.
But when he tried to get down from the horse . . .
he discovered he was stuck fast.
His wife pulled.
His sons pulled.
He would not come loose.
His bottom was stuck fast.
Then he remembered the little cricket.
  "Allah must have heard her call," he said.
  "I had better go find the mouse.
  But how will I find a mouse in this city?"

He began to ride up one street and down the other
calling into every shop,
  "Uncle! Have you seen a mouse?
  O Uncle! Did a mouse come in here?"
After a while he gave up and just rode through the streets calling,
  "Mouse! Mouse!
  The Lady of the House
  into the water fell!"

At last he passed the soap shop.
The mouse was just buying his soap.

When he heard the horseman's call he knew at once that the message
was for him.

"My wife! My wife!
She must be in danger!"

He put the soap in his pocket and ran quickly from the town to rescue
his little wife.

Now as soon as the mouse heard this message,
the man's bottom came unstuck from his horse.
"The mouse must have heard," he said and climbed gratefully down
from his horse.

The mouse ran to his wife.
"Here, little wife . . .
Grab on to my ears and I will pull you out."
But she could not reach his ears.

"Grab on to my paws and I will pull you out."
But she could not reach his paws.

"What will I do? What can I do?"
And then remembered his tail.

"Here, little wife . . .
Grab on to my tail and I will pull you out."
And he dangled his tail in the water.
Little Cricket pulled herself out of the hole.

"Look what you've done!" she cried.

"You went off and left me
and I fell into the sea!"
"Never mind," said he.
"I won't leave you again.
Let's do our laundry."

So they washed all of their clothing
and spread it in the sun to dry.
Then they each took a bath,
being careful not to fall into the water.

They folded their laundry
and went back to their home.
Mr. Mouse in front, "Tzee . . . tzee . . . tzee . . ."
and Little Cricket behind, "Tzee . . . tzee . . . tzee . . ."

And that is the end of their story.
Unless, of course, they had another pile of dirty laundry the next
    week. . . .

NOTES ON TELLING

This little cricket is very spunky. When aggravated she tells the larger animal, "Cricket, cricket your MOTHER!" and goes on with further unprintable insults in the variant collected by Muhawi and Kanaana, which is mentioned below. I changed this to "Cricket, cricket yourself!" for the printed tale, but must admit that I often resort to "Cricket, cricket your MAMA!" in telling.

I like to play with the audience as I tell, asking someone on one side of the room to "place your money in my sleeve, and I'll go ask my momma," and then crossing the room, "tzee . . . tzee . . . tzee," to address a lady on the other side of the room as if she were my "momma."

This is actually two separate stories. The "Ms. Cricket Takes a Husband" segment can be told alone if a shorter story is needed, or the story can be told in two installments.

66

COMPARATIVE NOTES

This tale is found in *Speak, Bird, Speak Again: Palestinian Arab Folktales* by Ibrahim Muhawi and Sharif Kanaana (p. 199). Other variants are found in Stephan H. Stephan's "Palestinian Animal Stories and Fables" in the *Journal of the Palestine Oriental Society* (III, 4: 181). Muhawi and Kanaana cite several Palestinian variants of this tale in their tale notes, along with variants from Syria and Iraq. The protagonist is sometimes a black beetle or scarab beetle. They note that in the Iraqi versions the mouse falls into a jar of honey and drowns at the tale's end.

A delightful variant from Iraq, "The Scarab Beetle's Daughter," is found in *Arab Folktales,* collected by Inea Bushnaq (p. 225–227). When the mouse turns around and dangles his tail in the water to rescue his drowning wife, he is in a quandary, because to turn one's back on someone is rude in Arab society. For this reason, in some versions he dangles another part of his anatomy for her to grab hold and pull herself up.

This tale is Type 2023 (also Motif Z37.3) *Little Ant Finds a Penny, Buys New Clothes with It, and Sits in Her Doorway.* The variant best known to American children appears in the picture book *Perez and Martina,* by Pura Belpré. My *Storyteller's Sourcebook* cites sources from Mexico, Persia, Portugal, Puerto Rico, Spain, and Turkey. A tragic ending, in which the mouse falls in a pot of soup and drowns, is common to most of these tales. That ending alone, without the wedding motif, appears as a cumulative tale in British and German folklore (MacDonald, Motif Z32.2.2).

PLEASE ALL . . . PLEASE NONE

There was once a proud miller who wanted everyone to think well of
    him.
One day the miller and his son took their donkey to town.
The miller planned to sell the donkey for a good price.

Down the road they went.
The miller first, striding proudly along.
Next the donkey, his head in the air.
    Clop . . . clop . . . clop. . . .
And last the son, walking briskly to keep up.

Along the way they passed a group of women washing clothes.
The women began to mutter among themselves.
        "Such a foolish man.

He has a fine strong donkey,
and yet he makes his poor son walk behind in the dust.
The son should ride on the donkey's back."

The miller stopped.
    "I never thought of that.
    I suppose they must be right.

    "Son, get up on the donkey and ride."

So the boy climbed up on the donkey's back.
Down the road they went.
The miller striding proudly ahead;
the donkey with the son on his back clopping along,
but not so lightly as before.
    clop . . . clop . . . clop. . . .

They passed a group of men chopping wood.
The men stopped and stared.
They began to criticize.
    "What a lazy good-for-nothing boy,
    riding while his father must walk in the dust.
    Shame on you, sir, for spoiling your son that way.
    You should ride and he should walk."

The miller stopped.
    "I never thought of that.
    I suppose they must be right.

    "Son, get down.
    I will ride the donkey."

69

So the son got down
and the father climbed onto the donkey's back.
Down the road they went.
The father riding on the donkey.
The donkey clopping unhappily along.
　　Clop . . . clop . . . clop. . . .
The son trudging behind in the dust.

They passed an old woman spreading her laundry to dry.
The woman began to scold.
　　　　"Look at that lazy man.
　　　　See how he rides, while his son must walk behind.
　　　　He should be ashamed.
　　　　Why doesn't he take the son up and let him ride with him?"

The miller stopped.
　　　　"I never thought of that.
　　　　I suppose she must be right.

　　　　"Son, climb up behind me.
　　　　We can both ride the donkey."

So the son climbed up behind the father.
The poor donkey was now so loaded that his back sagged under their
　　weight.
Down the road they went.
The father riding the donkey.
The son riding the donkey.
The donkey clopping angrily along.
　　CLOP . . . CLOP . . . CLOP. . . .

They met an old man.

"Shame! Shame!" fussed the old man.

"Shame on you for loading your poor donkey down this way.

If you plan to sell him at market you are mistaken.

He will not be worth a cent by the time you get him there.

Better you should carry HIM than that he should have to carry
you both."

The miller stopped.

"I never thought of that.

I suppose he must be right.

"Son, get down.

We will carry the donkey."

So the miller and his son climbed off the donkey.

The miller cut a sturdy pole.

They tied the donkey's four legs to the pole,

hoisted the pole over their shoulders,

and trudged down the road

carrying the donkey.

Down the road they went.

The miller first, trudging along.

The son behind, staggering under the weight.

And the poor donkey swaying upside down from the pole between
them, braying in terror.

When they reached the town everyone stopped to laugh at this absurd
sight.

The donkey in its fright began to struggle even harder.
Just as they reached the town bridge, the donkey broke loose.
The donkey fell to the bridge,
leaped over the railing,
and swam away down the river.

The miller and his son stood staring after their donkey.
   "What a bad day," said the miller.
   "I did just what everyone said I should do.
   And look what happened.
   I tried to please everybody.
   But I pleased no one.
   Not even myself."

So the miller and his son turned and began the long walk home.
Up the road they went,
dragging their feet sadly.

The moral of this story is:
   Please all . . . please none.

NOTES ON TELLING

Invite the children to swing their arms with the father as he strides, make fists and clop on their knees with the donkey, and huff and puff as the son runs behind. The sequence should be rhythmical:

   The miller first, striding proudly along.
     (stride . . . stride . . . stride . . .)
   Next the donkey, his head in the air.
     (clop . . . clop . . . clop . . .)
   And last the son, walking briskly to keep up.
     (huff . . . huff . . . huff . . .)

72

The donkey's clops get heavier and heavier as his load increases throughout the story.

As the story ends with the sound of the father and son trudging home, rub your palms on your legs to make a trudging sound. (trudge . . . trudge . . . trudge . . .)

I prepared this retelling of the Aesop tale for use by actor Billy Seago in his sign-language video "The Father, The Son, and the Donkey" (Sign-a-Vision, 1986, P.O. Box 30580, Seattle, Washington 98103-0580). Watching Billy's dramatic telling may give you ideas for your own rendition.

COMPARATIVE NOTES

Motif J1041.2 *The miller, his son and the ass: trying to please everyone* is one of Aesop's best known fables, for which my *Storyteller's Sourcebook* cites sixteen sources. For slightly different variants, see the Turkish tale in *Tales of the Hodja* by Charles Downing (p. 21) and the Taiwanese tale in Cora Cheney's *Tales from a Taiwanese Kitchen* (p. 133–136). For an interesting twist on the tale, see the Yoruba story in Harold Courlander and Ezekiel Eshugbayi's *Olode the Hunter* (p. 65–68). In this Yoruba variant, Ologbon-Ori and his son visit various towns on a camel, seeking wisdom. They find the wisdom of one town is the stupidity of another.

WHY KOALA HAS NO TAIL

This is an Australian story of Koala and Tree Kangaroo.

Tree Kangaroo is smaller than his cousins.
He has feet shaped in a special way so that he can climb trees.

There was a time when no rain fell for many days.
Everything became very dry.
Even the streams had dried up.
Only dry streambeds were left.

Koala and Tree Kangaroo were so thirsty.
They searched everywhere but could not find a drop of water to
    drink.
But one day Tree Kangaroo remembered something.

"When I was just a baby there was a dry time like this.
My mother went to a certain dry stream bed.
She dug a deep hole.
Water seeped into the bottom of the hole.
There was not much water.
But there was enough for a sip for my mother and a sip for
me."

Koala was excited.
"Do you think you could find that place again?"

"I think so," said Tree Kangaroo.
"Then let's go there," said Koala.
"Let's go NOW."

Koala and Tree Kangaroo walked and walked.
They came to a dry streambed.
"Is this the place?" asked Koala.
Tree Kangaroo looked around.
"No. This isn't the place."

Koala and Tree Kangaroo walked and walked.
They came to another dry streambed.
"Is this the place?" asked Koala.
Tree Kangaroo looked around.
"No. This isn't the place."

Koala and Tree Kangaroo walked and walked.
It was such a long way.
They came to another dry streambed.
"Is this the place?" asked Koala.

Tree Kangaroo looked around.
He looked at everything carefully.
"Yes! This is the place!"

"Then let's begin to dig!"
Koala sat down.
"I'm such a small animal.
The walk has made me tired.
Why don't you dig first, Tree Kangaroo."

So Tree Kangaroo began to dig.
He dug and he dug.
He threw out gravel.
He dug and he dug.
It was very hot.
He dug and he dug.
He got so tired.

"I'm tired, Koala.
You take a turn now."

But when Tree Kangaroo looked for Koala
he saw him curled up in the shade
with his long tail over his eyes.
Koala looked so tired.

"I'll let him rest a little longer," thought Tree Kangaroo.
And Tree Kangaroo began to dig again.
He dug and he dug.
He threw out gravel.

He dug and he dug.
He was very hot.
He dug and he dug.
He got so tired.

"Your turn, Koala.
I've had two turns now.
You dig for a while."

Koala woke up.
"I'm coming.
I want to help.

"OH! I've got a thorn in my tail!
I can't dig yet.
You go ahead."

So Tree Kangaroo dug some more.
He dug and he dug.
He threw out gravel.
He dug and he dug.
He was very hot.
He dug and he dug.
He got so tired.

"You take a turn now, Koala.
I've had three turns.
It's your turn to dig."

"I'm coming," said Koala.
"I want to help.

"OH! I just got a cramp in my tail!
You'd better dig a bit more.
I'll be there as soon as the cramp goes away."

So Tree Kangaroo dug some more.
He dug and he dug.
He threw out dirt.
He dug and he dug.
He was very hot.
He dug and he dug.
He got so tired.

"Koala, come dig.
I've had four turns now.
It is your turn."

Koala came over and looked into the hole.
"It is almost deep enough.
After all that work, you should have the pleasure of finding
the water.
Just go ahead and finish."

Koala sat down to wait.

Tree Kangaroo started to dig again.
He dug and he dug.
He threw out dirt.
He dug and he dug.
He was very hot.
He dug and he dug.
He got so tired.

Then . . .
water began to seep into the hole.

"Koala! I did it!
There is almost enough for one sip already.
In a moment there will be enough for both of us to drink!"

Koala jumped up.
He shoved Tree Kangaroo out of the hole.
Koala hopped into the hole
and began to drink up that water.

Koala was head down in that hole,
slurping up all of the water.
His foolish tail stuck straight up out of the hole as he drank.

Tree Kangaroo was so angry.
He looked at that tail.
"Swoosh!" He pulled it right off.

"Owwww" Koala came out of the hole.
He looked at Tree Kangaroo.
Tree Kangaroo looked at him.
But Koala didn't say a word.

He knew he had been lazy.
He knew he had been greedy.
He knew he had taken advantage of Tree Kangaroo.

Koala's tail never did grow back.
To this day all koalas are without tails—

a reminder of the koala who was lazy and greedy,
the koala who took advantage of his friend.

NOTES ON TELLING

The audience will help you dig for water, tossing the gravel over their shoulders and wiping their brows as they get hotter and hotter.

COMPARATIVE NOTES

This story is based on "Why Koala Has No Tail" in *Aboriginal Legends: Animal Tales* by A. W. Reed (p. 41–44).

That tale includes an elaborate embedded story of the sacrifice of Tree Kangaroo's mother in her attempts to find water and save her child. Stith Thompson's Motif A2233.1.1 *Animals refuse to help dig well: may not drink from river or spring* cites variants from Estonia, Livonia, and Lithuania. This is also Type 55 *The Animals Build a Road (Well),* in which the fox as overseer punishes lazy animals. My *Storyteller's Sourcebook* cites numerous variants of A2233.1.1: Cherokee, Congo, Thonga, African-American, and others.

KATCHI KATCHI BLUE JAY

When the world was new
the moon came up every night.
It crossed the sky and made light for the animals.
Those animals who move at night were pleased with this.
The moon made light so they could see to hunt food
and go about their business.

But one night the moon did not come up.
The animals waited . . .
but the night remained dark.

Something must be done.
The chief called the animals together.
       "The moon must have overslept tonight.

It is too dark.
Nobody can see a thing.
We need someone to go and wake the moon.

"But it must be someone fast.
We need help quickly.
It must be someone strong.
It is a long way to the moon's house.
And it must be someone smart.
The moon has a clapping door.
It claps shut and snatches anyone who tries to enter."

When the chief said "swift" and "strong" and "smart,"
Blue Jay jumped up.
"That would be ME!
You said 'fast'?
That's ME.
You said 'strong'?
That sounds like ME.
You said 'smart'?
That's ME all right.
I'm the one you need."

"Well you can go then, Blue Jay.
But come sit here by me for a moment.
I will give you some advice about that clapping door."

"I'm in a hurry.
I don't have time for advice.
I'm fast.

I'm strong.
I'm smart.
I'll get through that door."

And Blue Jay flew off.

Now Blue Jay did have a plan.
He flew to the top of the tallest tree he could see.
Then from the top of that tree he spotted an even taller tree.
He flew to the top of that tree.
And from that tree he could see an even taller tree.
So he flew to the top of that tree.

And so
flying to ever higher trees
he made his way up the mountain.

At last Blue Jay came to the top of the tallest tree
on the tallest mountain.

And when he landed, he bumped into something soft and feathery.
And that something said, "Whooooo?"

It was the owl who lives at the top of the tallest tree,
on the top of the tallest mountain.

  "Whooooo?"
  "It's ME," said Blue Jay.
  "I'm on my way to Moon's house.
  He didn't wake up tonight.
  No one can see anything."

"Yes, I noticed," said Owl.
"You just bumped into me."
"Well, I'm in a hurry," said Blue Jay.
"I have to get to Moon's house."

"Come sit by me a moment," said Owl.
"I'll give you a bit of advice
about Moon's clapping door."

"I don't have time for ADVICE," said Blue Jay.
"I'm in a hurry.
I'm fast.
I'm strong.
I'm smart.
I won't need advice."

From the top of this tallest tree
on this tallest mountain
Blue Jay could just see Moon's house up in the sky.

He took his strongest, fastest leap
and he landed right in Moon's front yard.

But Moon's house DID have a clapping door.
It was opening . . .
and SHUTTING.
Opening . . .
and SHUTTING.
And every once in a while the door would open-shut-open-shut—
very rapidly.

"This may be harder than I thought," said Blue Jay.

Blue Jay gathered himself together.
He counted the door's rhythm.
Open . . .
SHUT.
Open . . .
SHUT.
Here I . . .
SHUT . . . GO!
open-shut!
BAM! The door had slammed on Blue Jay's head.

"Katchi! Katchi! Katchi!"
Blue Jay jumped around holding his poor head.
His head feathers were squished out in a silly topknot now, sticking
    straight out of his head.
And it hurt!
"Katchi! Katchi! Katchi!"

Jumping around like this and holding his head,
Blue Jay didn't see where he was going.
Moon's door . . . opened . . .
and Blue Jay stumbled right through without even knowing.

"Katchi! Katchi! Katchi!"
Now Blue Jay was hopping around on Moon's floor.
Moon woke up and sat up in bed.
    "WHAT is this little blue bird doing?
    Why is he hopping around on my floor making this
    'Katchi! Katchi! Katchi!' racket?"

Blue Jay looked up.
"You must be the moon!
Look what your silly door did to my head!
Katchi! Katchi! Katchi!
My chief sent me to wake you up.
And look what your door did.
Katchi! Katchi! Katchi!"

"Now wait a minute," said the moon.
"Didn't your chief give you any advice about how to get
    through my door?"

"Oh, ADVICE.
I didn't have time to listen to any advice."

"I see," said the moon.
"But on the way you must have passed the owl who lives on
    the top of the tallest tree on the tallest mountain.
Didn't HE give you advice about my door?"

"Oh, I was in a hurry," said Blue Jay.
I didn't have time to listen to HIM."

"I see," said Moon.
"Well, Blue Jay, I think you need to learn a lesson.
You need to learn to listen to the advice of your elders.

From now on you will just keep that silly ruff of feathers
    sticking out of your head.
When anyone sees that silly topknot

they will remember this:
ALWAYS LISTEN TO THE ADVICE OF YOUR ELDERS."

"Oh, Katchi! Katchi! Katchi!," said Blue Jay.
"It's all YOUR fault anyway.
If you hadn't overslept I wouldn't have had to come wake you
up."

"I don't like your tone of voice," said Moon.
"Don't you know you should speak respectfully to your
elders?
I am your elder.
And you are not speaking very respectfully.

"From now on
you will just say one thing,
'Katchi! Katchi! Katchi!'

"When anyone hears your
'Katchi! Katchi! Katchi!'
they will remember this:
ALWAYS SPEAK RESPECTFULLY TO YOUR ELDERS."

"Katchi! Katchi! Katchi!," said Blue Jay.
And that was all he could say.

"Now don't come waking me up again," said Moon.
"I am allowed to sleep in one night every month.
Haven't you ever heard of the DARK OF THE MOON?
Well, this is it."

87

Moon held the door open for Blue Jay.
And Blue Jay flew back down to the earth
crying, "Katchi . . . katchi . . . katchi. . ."

If you see Blue Jay today,
you will notice his silly topknot sticking straight up
and you will remember that you should . . .
   ALWAYS LISTEN TO THE ADVICE OF YOUR ELDERS.

And when you hear him calling in that hoarse, disrespectful voice,
   "Katchi . . . katchi . . . katchi . . ."
You will remember that you should . . .
   ALWAYS SPEAK WITH RESPECT TO YOUR ELDERS.

NOTES ON TELLING

After the dramatic pause at the story's end has passed, ask if anyone knows what advice the chief and Owl might have given Blue Jay, had he taken time to listen. The audience will suggest magic words, knocking, flying over. Hint that the chief and owl knew a way to keep the door open. Someone almost always thinks of putting a rock or a stick in the door to hold it open. That is the correct answer. The chief and Owl *would* have told Blue Jay to take a stick along and put it in the door to hold it open. This information is actually part of the story, but I find it works best dramatically when used as a follow-up. In one version Moon whittles a point on a stick, gives it to Blue Jay to prop the door open so he can get out, and tells him that this is the advice he would have been given, had he listened.

    The business about the dark of the moon is my own addition. The Nisqually legend from which I was working just said that the moon had permission to rise later that night.

COMPARATIVE NOTES

This is related to Motif D1553 *Symplegades. Rocks that clash together at intervals.* The Symplegades are encountered by Jason and the Argonauts and are floating cliffs that crash together when anything attempts to pass between them. A motif of clapping mountains is found in Eskimo tales collected by Charles Gilham in *Beyond the Clapping Mountains* (p. 1, 31) and in Helen Caswell's *Shadows from the Singing House* (p. 64). In a Peruvian tale compiled by Moritz Jagendorf in *King of the Mountain* (p. 238), a father rescues his daughter from a witch who keeps her imprisoned behind clashing rocks.

The clashing rocks motif is cited by Stith Thompson in *Tales of the North American Indians* (p. 275) as appearing in twelve northwest coast groups as well as in Miwok, Cahuilla, Shoshoni, Crow, Assiniboin, Seneca, Cherokee, Yuchi, Navaho, Apache, and Eskimo tales. The specific motif of a snapping door (K736) appears in Nass, Bella Bella, Bella Coola, Thompson, Kwakiutl, Newette Rivers Inlet, Nootka, Comax, Squamish, Tilamook, and Tsmimshian tales.

This version is based on a Nisqually tale remembered by Paul Leschi and compiled by Emerson N. Matson in *Legends of the Great Chiefs* (p. 28). Matson notes, "Blue jays were common to the area, and inhabited the brush surrounding Nisqually villages. Every time the jays would scream, 'Katchi, Katchi,' the children were reminded to listen to advice and to speak with respect."

THE BIYERA WELL

Once a donkey, a goat, and a duck became partners.
      "What kind of crop shall we plant?"
      "Let's plant CLOVER."

So they planted a field of clover.
The three worked very hard.
They prepared the soil.
They planted the seeds.
They watered the young plants.
They weeded the field.
They tended that clover for several weeks.
At last, the clover was SO high.

      "Quack, quack," said Duck.
      "Tomorrow we eat our clover!"

"Baa, baa," said Goat.
"Tomorrow we eat our clover!"

"Eeehaw, eeehaw," said Donkey.
"Tomorrow we eat our clover!"

The animals went home and went to bed.

Duck fell asleep and began to dream about the clover.
Duck dreamed it tasted so sweet, so good.

Goat fell asleep and began to dream about the clover.
Goat dreamed it tasted so sweet, so good.

But Donkey didn't fall asleep.
Donkey lay awake and THOUGHT about the clover.
He could imagine that field of clover lying there in the moonlight.
He could imagine the sweet scent of it on the breeze.
In the middle of the night the donkey got up.
He went out to the field.
He landed right in the middle of the field and began
        hatatak . . . hatatak . . .
        hatatak . . . hatatak . . .
        hatatak . . . hatatak . . .

Down one side and up the other
that donkey munched and munched.
What did he do?
He ate it ALL.

And then
he found he could hardly MOVE!
His belly was THAT high.
Home he crawled and into bed.

In the morning the goat and the duck went to wake the donkey.
>"Today is the DAY.
>
>Let's go eat our CLOVER!"

But the donkey was very sick.
>"I feel so ill this morning.
>
>Go ahead without me.
>
>Just eat your share and leave mine.
>
>I'll eat it later."

So the goat and the duck went out to the field.
>"What was this!
>
>Where is the CLOVER?
>
>There is NO CLOVER!
>
>No one could have done this but . . .
>>the DONKEY."

They hurried home.
>"I didn't eat it," said the donkey.
>
>"Well I didn't eat it," said the goat.
>
>"And I didn't eat it," said the duck.
>
>"Then WHO?"
>
>"Let us all go to the Biyera Well and swear by it."

So they went.

First came the duck.
>"Quack. Quack. If I've eaten it.
>
>Quack. Quack. If I've drunk it.
>
>Quack. Quack. Biyera Well may I fall in you.
>
>And remain there for two months and one night."

And the duck jumped to the other side.

Duck jumped right across the Biyera Well
and did not fall in.

Next came Goat.
>"Baa. Baa. If I've eaten it.
>Baa. Baa. If I've drunk it.
>Baa. Baa. Biyera Well may I fall in you.
>And remain there for two months and one night."

And Goat jumped to the other side.

Last came the Donkey.
>"Eeehaw. Eeehaw. If I've eaten it.
>Eeehaw. Eeehaw. If I've drunk it.
>Eeehaw. Eeehaw. Biyera Well may I fall in you.
>And remain there for two months and one night."

Then that donkey tried to jump.
But his belly was SO heavy.
Down he fell into Biyera Well.
And there he remained for two months and one night.

He who swears falsely
falls in the end.

NOTES ON TELLING

This piece is so short that you may not want to use audience participation on the first telling. On subsequent tellings the children will want to join on the animals' chants. To use this as creative dramatic play, just add more animals to the crew.

COMPARATIVE NOTES

This is based on a tale collected by Hasan M. El-Shamy in *Folktales of Egypt*. He notes that he recorded the tale March 9, 1969 from eleven-year-old Nadya Seliman. She had heard the story from her father, and he prompted her during her telling. The father would not tell the story himself as it was "for children only." He had learned the tale from his mother. El-Shamy explains that in actual life swearing as a testimony of truth should be only "by God," though other types of oaths appear in folk culture. Wells with supernatural powers are a common folk theme in Egypt, some have jinn or other supernatural beings living in them.

In another Egyptian version collected by Hamed Ammar (*Growing Up in an Egyptian Village*, p. 168) a goat, cock, and donkey farm together. The donkey cries "hee-haw" while jumping the well and is grabbed by a wolf lying in wait in the well.

This tale, Type 136A *Confession of Animals,* is related to Type 44 *The Oath on the Iron*, and bears similarity to Type 15 *The Theft of Butter (Honey) by Playing Godfather*. For many variants of Type 15 see MacDonald K372 *Playing Godfather*. The tale also features Motif H220 *Ordeals. Guilt or innocence thus established.* For an extensive discussion of this tale and its variants throughout the Middle East and Africa see El-Shamy's notes in *Folktales of Egypt* (p. 294–296). He states that this is one of the most popular animal tales in Egypt and cites sources from Tunisia, Palestine, Iraq, and Sudan. He describes a Bantu tale, included in Edouard Jacottet's *The Treasury of Ba-Suto Lore,* in which a chief's wives are made to walk a rope stretched across a pool, the one guilty of eating the chief's tortoise will fall. In a Bene-Mukuni variant, family members must walk a rope across a river, the one guilty of eating the father's guinea fowl will fall (in James Torrend's *Specimens of Bantu Folklore from Northern Rhodesia*). El-Shamy cites variants also from Tanzania (Safwa), Kenya (Kamba), Nigeria (Hausa and Ibo). In an Anancy tale from the West Indies, Nancy, Bro' Toukouma, and Bro' Lion harvest sugar-apples. Nancy eats them and all are tested by jumping over a fire. They sing "Sillee sillee da mande. . . . Oh hole your back, da mande. . . . Tie your buby no bal-crim" and jump. Nancy falls and is scorched. (This version is cited in "Folk-Lore from Antigua, British West Indies" by John H. Johnson in *Journal of American Folk-Lore* 34, no. 131 [1921]: 46–48.)

El-Shamy notes that in Ancient Egyptian belief a Pool of Justice was found in the hereafter. Sinners would fail to cross it safely. In modern Islamic tradition *sirat*, a path bridging hell and leading to paradise, must be crossed and sinners will fall off into hell.

THE STRAWBERRIES OF THE LITTLE MEN

There was once a little boy and a little girl.
They lived in a poor little hut
and they never had enough to eat.
But their granny taught them good manners
and people liked them for it.

Folks in the village would give them a bit of food now and then,
a cabbage leaf or two,
a turnip for their pot,
a bone for their soup,
or a crust of leftover bread.

The children were never greedy.
They always took just enough to satisfy their hunger and never more.

"That's enough to go on with, thank you kindly," they would say.
Because they were such polite children and not at all greedy, people
were glad to share with them.

Now, their little goat did not give much milk.
A goat must have good green grass to eat, if it is to give rich milk,
and the goat had long ago eaten up all of the grass in their yard.

So each day, the boy and girl took the goat out along the road in search
of grass to nibble.
Even then, the poor little goat could give only enough milk at night for
each of them to have one sip.

Down the road was the rich man's house.
He had fine orchards
and corn ricks
and a herd of cows,
but he sold every cabbage leaf
and he counted every turnip
and he never gave away a bone or a crust of bread.

Whenever he saw the two children and their little goat coming,
he would run into his yard shaking his fist.
"Get out of here!
Move along!
That's MY grass.
Don't let your goat nibble MY grass."
And he would set his dog to barking at them.
So they always hurried on past.

One day they went so far in search of grass that they came to the Wood
of the Little Men.

The children knew that no one was allowed in THAT wood.

But the little goat suddenly broke loose and ran right into the woods,
where the grass grew thick.

The children could not see the Little Men, but they knew they were
there.

And they knew the Little Men did not like intruders.

The children were frightened, but they remembered their manners.

"Little Men, our goat has gone into your woods," they called.

"We must go catch her.

Pardon us.

Thank you kindly."

And in they ran after the goat.

They found that little goat
standing in a clearing and nibbling—
not grass—
but red ripe STRAWBERRIES!

The ground was covered with strawberries!

These were the magic strawberries of the Little Men.

And if anyone ate them, that was fine.

IF they said "please"
and IF they knew when to stop eating.

But if they did NOT—

why, they would just have to keep eating and eating
until the Little Men decided they could stop.

And here was the little goat
gobbling away
without so much as a "by your leave" or "thank you."

     "Oh forgive our goat!" cried the children.
     "May he eat your strawberries?
     Thank you kindly!"

When they saw how ripe and good those strawberries looked,
the children just had to taste them too.

     "Please may we taste your strawberries?" they called.
     "Thank you kindly."
     And they both started to eat.

Now, the Little Men were watching from among the trees.
     They snickered when they saw the children begin to eat.
     "They will soon be gobbling like every other greedy body
        who comes here," they thought.
But the children ate only just enough to satisfy their hunger and then
    they stopped.
     "That's enough, thank you," they called.
     "That's enough to be going on with. Thank you kindly!"

And then they thought of their granny at home.
     "Could we pick a wee handful for our granny at home?
     She hasn't had strawberries for such a long time.
     Thank you kindly!"
And each picked just a wee handful for their granny.

98

Then they took their goat
and home they went.

"Well, what polite children!" said the Little Men.
"We must do something for them."

When the children reached home they ran into their yard.
"Granny! Granny! Look what we've found!"
But those mischievous Little Men put a magic on them
and they tripped over their feet
and fell onto the lawn,
spilling strawberries everywhere!

"Oh! No!"

But each strawberry that fell
put down roots and began to grow into a strawberry plant.
And the plants began to spread.
Soon the yard was covered with ripe red strawberries.
This was a gift from the Little Men.

From that day their yard was red with ripe strawberries all the
    year long.
Not only in summer . . . but even in winter when snow
    covered the ground.

One cold winter day, the mean old rich man passed by.
"Where did those strawberries come from?" he yelled.
"These must be MY strawberries, that I grew to SELL."
And that was a LIE.

"Give me back my berries!"
The rich man began to grab berries by the handful and eat them.

The little boy and little girl just watched.
They knew more berries would grow when the mean man had left.

Soon he had eaten every berry in the yard.
"Is that all there is?
I want MORE!"

"Well, there are more strawberries in the Wood of the Little
Men," they said.
"But be sure to say "please" and . . ."
The rich man had raced off down the road without paying a bit of
attention to what they said.

Into the Wood of the Little Men he ran.
And he began to gobble strawberries.
And he ate and he ate . . . and he didn't say "please."
And he ate and he ate . . . and he didn't say "that's enough."
And he ate and he ate . . . and he didn't say "thank you."
And he ate and he ate . . .
and he COULDN'T STOP EATING!

The Little Men had put their spell on the greedy man and all he could
do was eat and eat.
He ate all day.
He ate all Monday.
He ate all Tuesday.
He ate all Wednesday.
He ate all Thursday.

He ate all Friday.

He ate all Saturday. . . .

And he grew as big and red as a ripe strawberry himself.

And when Sunday came . . .

    why he BURST WITH A BANG!

So that was the end of the greedy rich man . . .

who didn't say "please"

and didn't say "that's enough"

and didn't say "thank you!"

NOTES ON TELLING

This tale, with its explicitly didactic tone, might not be for every teller. It may help to think of the British nanny mentioned in our "COMPARATIVE NOTES", below, who used this tale both to delight and indoctrinate her charges. She need only quote it later to remind the children of their duty to say, "thank you," and to take only a modest amount when offered goodies.

    I tell this story without much audience participation, though some audiences like to chime in on the names of the weekdays at the tale's end.

    The "strawberries in the snow" image makes this a pleasant mid-winter tale.

COMPARATIVE NOTES

This is based on a tale included in *A Dictionary of British Folk-tales* by Katharine M. Briggs (p. 505–506). The tale was collected by Ruth L. Tongue in 1917 and she recalled that it came, "From the mother of a schoolfellow who had died. It was sent to me in a letter. They lived in the Charltons area and this tale was told by their gardener's wife, who had been their nanny. Rosie [the school friend] had always loved it and laughed at it, and quoted it."

    This is one of the many tales about just rewards for the kind and the unkind. For more such tales see Motif Q.2 *Kind and unkind girls* and Motif J2415 *Foolish imitation of lucky man* in my *Storyteller's Sourcebook*. Motif Q41 *Politeness rewarded* appears also in

101

another tale in Brigg's collection, "The Spring of the Sixpence," in which fairy gold from pixies may be kept after they are thanked politely. This thanking may be a didactic representation of nannies' attempts to train their charges. A probably more common theme is that of the tabu on thanking the fairy: Motif F348.10 *Tabu: mortal for whom fairy works must not thank fairy,* and Motif F381.3 *Fairy leaves when he is given clothes.*

THE ELK AND THE WREN

A Makah Tale, as told by Makah Elder Hildred Ides.

This is the story of the elk and the wren.
Wren is a little brown bird. Very tiny.
Elk is a huge animal.
Elk was King of the Woods around there.

The little wren came out one beautiful day.
She was happy.
She was singing.

> "Ee-ee-mah-way sa-sin-a-way
> Ka-wai ka-wai sa-sin-a-way
> Toom Toom"

And this irritated the elk.
He said, "Quiet there!
      You make too much noise!"

      "Oh, I'll sing if I want to!"
And she went right on singing.
      "Ee-ee-mah-way sa-sin-a-way
      Ka-wai ka-wai sa-sin-a-way
      Toom Toom"

      "If you don't stop that noise I'm coming out there."

      "Oh, you can't do anything to me."
And she continued to sing.
She was dancing all around.
      "Ee-ee-mah-way sa-sin-a-way
      Ka-wai ka-wai sa-sin-a-way
      Toom Toom"

The elk was getting very angry.
He threatened her.
      "If you don't stop that noise
      I can stomp on you with my hoof.
      I'll SMASH you."

      "You just try it.
      I can fly up your NOSE."

She continued to sing.
And sing.
      "Ee-ee-mah-way sa-sin-a-way

104

> Ka-wai ka-wai sa-sin-a-way
> Toom Toom"

Elk became so irritated.
He came out.
His hooves were just flying.
He was going to JUMP on her.

But before he hit the ground,
wren was UP and flying
right up his NOSE!

Elk began to SNEEZE and SNEEZE.
And he SNEEZED and he SNEEZED.
Until he fell over
and collapsed.

Wren finally came out.
She said
> "You poor thing.
> I warned you.

> Don't go picking on little bitty people.
> Just because you're so big,
> it doesn't mean that you can be mean to just ANYBODY."

NOTES ON TELLING

Hildred Ides told this tale in a quiet, restrained manner. But she used a very spunky voice for little wren's retorts. And her eyes twinkled with delight at this tiny creature who flew up the nose of the authoritarian bully. I wondered if Hildred herself had had to fly up the nose of authority a time or two in her life. Wren's song was sung by Hildred to the following tune:

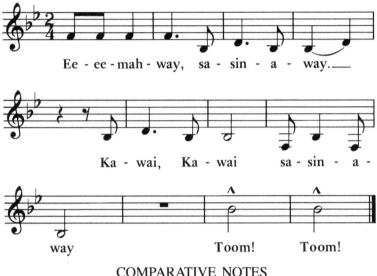

Ee - ee - mah - way,   sa - sin - a - way.___

Ka - wai,   Ka - wai   sa - sin - a -

way   Toom!   Toom!

COMPARATIVE NOTES

This story is set down as it was told by Makah elder Hildred Ides to an Elderhostel group at Penninsula College, Port Angeles, Washington in August of 1990. Permission to print the story was given after consultation with the Makah Cultural and Research Center at Neah Bay, Washington. The Makah Cultural and Research Center wishes it to be noted that the tribe thanks the author for requesting permission before publishing this material. Hildred asked that it be stressed that this is one tribal member's retelling of a tribal tale; others might tell the tale differently.

Helen Peterson, also of the Makah tribe, tells this story under the title "Too Proud Elk" on the album, *Songs and Stories from Neah Bay.*

The tale has parallels in the lore of several areas. Stith Thompson Motif L351.1 *Bird flies into large animal's ear and kills him* cites variants from Japan and Indonesia. L315.1.1 *Mouse runs into buffalo's ear and overcomes him* appears as a Congolese tale. As Type 228 *The Titmouse Tries to Be as Big as a Bear,* the titmouse ruffles up her feathers but does not succeed in fooling her young. But in her natural form, she flies into the bear's ear and kills him. Aarne-Thompson's *Types of the Folktale* lists variants from Finland, Estonia, Germany, Latvia, Russia, Greece, Indonesia, Africa, the West Indies, as well as a Franco-American variant.

THE BEAR-CHILD

Once there was an old couple who had no children of their own.

They were growing ever older, and the old man found it difficult to hunt
    for their needs.

One day, when he had killed an ice bear and was skinning it,
        he took some of the bear's fur and bones
        and he modeled a little bear from it.

When the old man had finished, he held the bear he had made and he
    began to chant:
        "Blood become flesh.
        Flesh become bone.
        Bone become fur.
        Ice bear, Ice bear.
        Come ALIVE for me."

And the small ice bear suddenly sprang to life.
It was a tiny ice-bear cub!
The old man took the bear cub home to his wife.
They petted the bear cub and fed it tidbits of their food.
At night they took it to bed with them under their warm sleeping skins.
They grew to love the little ice bear.

One day the old man said,
       "Let us adopt this little cub as our own bear-child."

They held the ice-bear cub and they said
       "Blood of OUR blood.
       Flesh of OUR flesh.
       Bear-child, Bear-child.
       You are our own child."

Every day the bear-child would go out to play with the other ice-bear
    children.
But in the evening the old man would call to him.
       "Blood of our blood.
       Flesh of our flesh.
       Bear-child, Bear-child.
       Come to us."

And the bear-child would come running across the ice.
The old man and old woman would hug the bear-child
and take it into their home.

One day the old man said to his wife,
       "I am growing ever weaker.

But our bear-child is growing ever stronger.
I wonder if he is strong enough to hunt for us?"

So he went out and called the bear-child to him.
"Blood of my blood.
Flesh of my flesh.
Bear-child, Bear-child.
Come to me."

The bear-child came running.
And the old man said,
"I am the house father
And you are my son.
Do you think you are old enough now
to hunt for us?"
And the bear-child nodded.

The bear-child went away
and that night he returned, carrying a salmon in his mouth.

The old man cut it up, and the old woman cooked it.
She put a piece of the salmon in front of the bear-child for his supper.
The bear-child nodded, and ate it.

After that, the bear-child would go out each day to hunt.
And in the evening he would bring back a salmon for their supper.

One morning the old man said to his wife,
"You know, our bear-child is growing ever stronger.
I believe he could kill a seal.

Then we would have oil for our lamps
and with the skins you could make new clothing."

He called the bear-child to him.
    "Blood of my blood.
    Flesh of my flesh.
    Bear-child, Bear-child.
    Come to me."

When the bear-child came
the old man said,
    "I am the house father
    And you are my son.
    Do you think you could hunt a seal for us?"

The bear-child nodded.

The bear-child went away.
And that night he returned, bringing a seal.

The old man cut it up.
The old woman fried it.
And she gave a piece to the bear-child for his supper.
The bear-child nodded, and ate it up.

Some time later, the old man said to his wife,
    "You know our bear-child is growing ever larger.
    I believe he is strong enough now to bring back a walrus.
    Then we would have plenty of blubber, and I could carve the
        tusks."

So he called the bear child to him.

    "Blood of my blood.

    Flesh of my flesh.

    Bear-child, Bear-child.

    Come to me."

And the bear-child came running over the ice.

    "I am the house father.

    And you are my son.

    You are almost fully grown.

    Do you think you are strong enough to kill a walrus for us?"

The bear-child thought a moment.

Then it nodded.

The bear-child went away.

And that night it returned, dragging a walrus.

The old man cut up the walrus.

The old woman cooked some of the meat.

And she placed it before the bear-child for his supper.

The bear-child nodded, and he ate it.

It was some months later that the old man said to his wife,

    "Wife, I am growing tired of this seafood and these sea
    animals which we eat.

    It has been a long time since we had some good bear steaks.

    Some fried bear meat would taste good.

    Our bear-child is now fully grown.

    I believe he could hunt an ice bear for us."

So the old man called to the bear-child.
    "Blood of my blood.
    Flesh of my flesh.
    Bear-child, Bear-child.
    Come to me."

The bear-child came running across the ice.
    "I am the house father
    And you are my son.
    You are fully grown now.
    You can do anything your house father could once do.
    Do you think you could hunt an ice bear for us?"

The bear-child did not want to disobey his father,
but the bear-child slowly shook his head.

    "I am the house father
    And you are my son.
    I ask you:
    Hunt an ice bear for us."

Again the bear-child shook his head.

Now, the old man loved the bear-child dearly.
But he could not understand the bear-child's feelings on this matter.
And so he said once more,
    "I am the *house father*
    And you are my son.
    I have raised you from a cub.
    I ask you now.
    Kill an ice bear for your family."

112

The bear-child slowly turned and walked off across the ice fields.

That night the bear-child returned,
dragging a dead ice bear.

The old man cut up the ice bear.
The old woman fried the ice-bear steaks.
And she put a portion of the ice-bear meat in front of the bear-child for
    his supper.
But the bear-child shook his head.
He would not eat.

The next morning when the old man and old woman awoke,
their house fire was out.
The house was cold.
And the bear-child was gone.

His tracks could be seen leading away over the ice.
They followed, calling him.
       "Blood of our blood.
       Flesh of our flesh.
       Bear-child, Bear-child.
       Come to us!"

But the bear-child did not return.

This is the story of an old man and an old woman who had no children
    of their own.
It is the story of the bear-child whom they came to love.
The bear-child whom they lost,
    because they could not understand.

NOTES ON TELLING

I thought this was an audience participation story for primary children when I learned it, but I soon realized that this was not the case. It is a very serious tale, and while some audiences join in the chant, the sort of playful audience participation that works with so many of our other tales is not appropriate here. This tale has deep meaning for upper-elementary and teen listeners. It is also a useful tale for parents to hear. The theme of the parent who fails to understand the true nature of his child touches all of our lives. Adoptive families may find this tale especially poignant.

COMPARATIVE NOTES

This tale is elaborated from a brief story in *A Kayak Full of Ghosts: Eskimo Tales,* gathered and retold by Lawrence Millman (p. 180–181). Millman states that the tale was told by Ken Annanack of Pangnirtung, Baffin Island "at the anniversary party for the big wind which took away his home, the local nursing station, the community garage, and half the Hudson Bay Store." In his introduction, Millman talks about listening to Annanack's stories in a tent, during another stormy night. Recording tales from Baffin Island and Greenland, the book offers an interesting glimpse of an earthy side of Eskimo telling not often anthologized.

TWO WOMEN HUNT FOR GROUND SQUIRRELS

In summertime Athabaskan women go up into the mountains to hunt for
    ground squirrels.
This is a ground-squirrel story.

Two women were hunting ground squirrels.
They went up in the mountains.
They built a little shelter to live in.
Every day they set their snares.
Every evening they checked them.
One woman caught big ground squirrels.
The other woman caught only small ground squirrels.
She was angry at the small size of those ground squirrels.
But she kept them anyway.
Just threw them in her basket to dry for winter food,
even though they were really too small to keep.

115

One day she saw a baby ground squirrel leg sticking out of her snare.

"Now it's BABY ground squirrels!
Why can't I catch big fat ground squirrels like my friend?"

She was so mad she snatched that baby ground squirrel out of the hole,
snare and all, and threw it into the brush.

Then she started walking away.

She walked and walked, fuming with anger.
Suddenly she realized she was walking in a fog.
It got very cold.
She felt wet all over.
She had lost her way.

She wandered and wandered in the fog,
feeling wetter and damper every minute.

Then she heard a voice.
"Shighinidu . . .Shighinidu . . .
Come here . . . come here . . .
Shighinidu . . . Shighinidu . . .
Come here . . . come here . . ."

She followed the singing
down the hill.
She felt her way with her walking stick.

Then she bumped into something.
She felt all around it.

It was a ground-squirrel house!
A big hummock of grass.

From inside the house she heard the voice singing.
       "Shighinidu . . . Shighinidu . . .
       Come in . . . come in . . .
       Shighinidu . . . Shighinidu . . .
       Come in . . . come in."

Then she heard,
       "Put your sleeve over your eyes,
       and lean your head against the house."

She put her sleeve over her eyes.
She leaned her head against the house . . .
And TUMBLED right inside!

She landed with a jolt.
That's what happened!

She sat up and opened her eyes.
She was inside a ground-squirrel house.
A fire was burning in the center of the floor.
She sat down and tried to warm herself.

There was a mother ground squirrel sitting on the bed,
   holding a ground-squirrel child in her lap.

This mother ground squirrel had been singing,
       "Nga-na . . . nga-na . . . come here . . . come here . . ."

Now she began to rock her child and sing to it sadly.

> "My little ground squirrel, little child . . .
> Why can't you stand up?
> My little ground squirrel, little child . . .
> Why can't you stand up?
> Vayula . . . vayula . . . vayula . . ."

The woman saw
a string was hanging down from the ground-squirrel child.
It was a snare, fastened around his waist.

Now she understood.
This was the baby ground squirrel she had heartlessly thrown away.

The woman went to the ground-squirrel mother.
She gently removed the snare from the child's waist.
When she pulled the snare loose the ground-squirrel child gasped,
> "Aaaaahhhh . . ."

The ground-squirrel mother looked at the woman.
> "You humans come here every summer.
> You are strangers. You don't know our ways.
> Please be more considerate.
> Do not be so cruel.
> Our children like to play.
> They keep running about.
> Don't be angry with them if they trip into your snares."

The ground-squirrel child looked up at her.
> "Nghuni . . . Nghuni . . . Ndaya!
> Nghuni . . . Nghuni . . . Ndaya!"

"I understand," said the woman.

"Now, you may go," said the ground-squirrel woman.

"Put your sleeve over your eyes, and lean your head against
    the wall again."

The woman put her sleeve up over her eyes.
She leaned her head against the wall . . .
and tumbled back outside.

The sun was shining.
The fog was gone.
She was standing in the meadow.

The woman started back along her snare lines.
In every snare she found a big ground squirrel.

From that time on, every summer this woman found big ground
    squirrels in her snares.
But if by accident a ground-squirrel child was caught,
She carefully unwound the snare and set it free.
She had learned from the ground-squirrel people how to behave.

This is what happened.
That is a ground-squirrel story.

NOTES ON TELLING

Though the mother ground squirrel's song is actually "Shighinidu nidaga," I have short-
ened it to "Shighinidu" so the children can chant with me on repeated tellings. It is likely
that this will be told without audience participation on the first telling, as it is a quiet story.

The tale fits units on social responsibility and conservation, as well as on kindness to animals.

COMPARATIVE NOTES

This is based on "Ground Squirrel" told by Antone Evans in *Dena'ina Sukdu'a: Traditional Stories of the Tanaina Athabaskans,* compiled by Joan M. Tenenbaum (p. 148–155). That edition contains the Dena'ina text for the tale, along with a handsome illustration by Dale DeArmond. The English translation is excellent and could be real aloud or memorized for telling. The ground-squirrel mother's song is given as:

Shighinidu nidaga   Shighinidu nidaga
sh-una yula   come to me,
una yula!   come!

Pertinent motifs are W10 *Kindness* and W155.1 *Hardness of heart.*

QUAIL SONG

There once was a boy who did not want to die.
        "I will never die," said this boy.
        "I will search for the Life-that-has-no-end."

        "This cannot succeed," said his mother.
        "All men must die.
        First you live on this earth.
        And when that time is finished
        you will live with the spirits of your grandfathers in the sky."

But the boy could not accept this.
He felt that if he could reach the sun,
    the sun might give him Life-that-has-no-end.

And so he started to walk.

For days and days he walked.
Always toward the sun.

For months . . .
for years . . .
he kept walking
toward the sun.

He crossed mountains.
He crossed plains.
Then he came to deserts.
He walked through forests.

And as he walked, he grew older.
He became a young man.
Then a middle-aged man.
And still . . . year after year
he walked toward the sun.

Always he looked straight ahead,
at the bright sun shining before him.

And he did get close to the sun.
But as he grew nearer, the sun's heat grew stronger
and the sun's rays were brighter.
And as he looked at that bright sun,
his eyes became dimmer and dimmer
until at last he could see nothing at all.

The boy-who-was-now-a-man was blind.

At last he had to admit that he would never reach the sun.
He would never find that Life-that-has-no-end.
He, like all living things, must one day die.
The boy-who-was-now-a-man turned to go back to his village.
But now he could not see.
He stumbled over rocks.
He fell against logs.
He crashed into trees.

Then it was that two quail brothers saw him.
They felt pity in their hearts for his efforts
and they came to help him.

One quail walked on each side.
And they called to him.

> "Come this way . . .
> come this way . . .
> come this way . . ."

First from one side came the call . . .
> "Come this way . . ."

Then from the other . . .
> "Come this way . . ."

So they led him slowly through the forests.
> "Come this way . . ."
> "Come this way . . ."

123

Across the deserts.
  "Come this way . . ."
  "Come this way . . ."

Across the plains.
  "Come this way . . ."
  "Come this way . . ."

Over the high mountains even.
  "Come this way . . ."
  "Come this way . . ."

Back to his own village they came.

But the trip took so long
that he was now an old, old man.

So he returned to tell his people,
  "My quest was a foolish one.
  It is true, as we have been taught,
  all men must die."

We do not forget the lesson this boy learned.
When we go to the fields we hear the tiny quail calling to us,
just as they called to him.
  "Come this way . . ."
  "Come this way . . ."
  "Come this way . . ."

And we remember.

NOTES ON TELLING

This is a quiet tale, though the audience may want to join softly on the quail's "come this way" in the closing moments of the story. I first told this as part of an end-of-life celebration for families remembering Adam Herbig, who had battled Ondine's Curse, a rare respiratory disease, for the brief year and a half of his life.

COMPARATIVE NOTES

This tale touches several motifs, A1335.1.0.1 *Origin of Death;* H1284 *Quest to the sun for answer to questions* (Type 400, 461); A2426.2 *Cries of birds;* and B151.2.0.3 *Bird shows way by singing.* This version is based on "Song of the Quail," a Cahuilla tale recorded in *A Thousand Years of American Indian Storytelling: A Weewish Tree Reader* by Jeanette Henry and Rupert Costo (p. 56–58). The teller of the tale is not noted. A musical score for the quail's song is provided.

Come this way... come this way... come this way...

125

GRANDFATHER BEAR IS HUNGRY

In the spring, when the warm sun began to shine on bear's cave,
Bear woke up and came out into the sunshine.
Ohhhhhh . . . he felt . . . HUNGRY!

Bear had not eaten a thing all winter long.
      "I am so HUNGRY!" growled Bear.
      "I am so HUNGRY!"

Bear lumbered down to the berry patch.
It was early in the spring.
The berries were not ripe yet.
      "I am so HUNGRY!" roared Bear.
      "I am so HUNGRY!"

Bear galumped down to the stream.
It was early in the spring.
The salmon were not running yet.
      "I am so HUNGRY!" howled Bear.
      "I am so HUNGRY!"

Bear stormed back into the forest.
He began to claw at a rotten tree stump.
But he could not find a single grub inside the stump.
      "I am so HUNGRY!
      I am so HUNGRY!"

Bear sat down.
He put his nose between his paws and he began to moan.
      "I am so HUNGRY!
      I am so HUNGRY!"

Tiny Chipmunk
lived under the stump.
He felt his house shaking and quaking.
He came scurrying out to see what was making such a commotion.

      "Grandfather Bear!
      What is going on?
      Why are you moaning so loudly?"

Grandfather Bear looked at the tiny animal.
      "I haven't eaten all winter and . . .
      I am so HUNGRY!"

Chipmunk cocked his head to one side and thought.
"I still have nuts and berries stored away in my burrow,
    Grandfather Bear.
I will share them with you!"
Chipmunk disappeared down his hole.
In a moment he was back with his cheeks full of nuts and driedberries.
Chipmunk dropped them in front of Grandfather Bear.

"HUNGRY!" said Grandfather Bear
and lapped up the little pile of nuts and berries.
Chipmunk ran back into his hole.
Back and forth,
back and forth,
all day Chipmunk ran,
carrying load after load of nuts and berries for Grandfather Bear.
His food was tiny, but gradually Grandfather Bear became full.

"Thank you, Chipmunk," said Grandfather Bear.
"You are a very small animal.
But you are kind."

Grandfather Bear reached out his huge paw.
He gently stroked his claws across the trembling back of the little
    chipmunk.
And where the claws passed
five black lines were left.

"Now you are handsome,"
    said Grandfather Bear.
"Whenever anyone sees you, Chipmunk,

They will notice your stripes,
and they will remember your kind heart."

So it is even today.
When you see tiny Chipmunk scurrying about
with his fine black stripes,
you will remember his kindness to Grandfather Bear.

NOTES ON TELLING

This brief story pleases me with its gentle bear and sharing chipmunk. Children will want to help you moan "I am so HUNGRY!" with Grandfather Bear. This is a good story to use right before snack time! And it is one that even the smallest listeners can enjoy. This is also great fun to act out using lots of chipmunks and lots of bears.

COMPARATIVE NOTES

Motif A2217.2 *Chipmunk's back scratched: hence his stripes.* This is a common Native American motif. My *Storyteller's Sourcebook* cites Iroquois, Nez Perce, and Creek variants, and Stith Thompson's *Motif-Index* cites Seneca variants. In those variants, however, as the chipmunk tries to escape, his back is scratched by Bear. This often occurs in conjunction with a contest over light. In a Crow tale, Chipmunk's back is scarred while trying to steal fire (MacDonald A1415.2.2.1.2), and in a California Native American tale Chipmunk's back is scratched by obsidian chips as he helps Blue Jay steal the dawn (MacDonald A721.1.2).

This Eiven story from the U.S.S.R. is unusual in that Bear scratches Chipmunk's back as a gift. The marks are a badge of pride, not a scar.

A version of this Eiven tale appears in *Northern Lights: Fairy Tales of the People of the North,* compiled by E. Pomerantseva, and translated by Irina Zheleznova (p. 32), and also in *Kutkha the Raven: Animal Stories of the North,* translated by Fainna Solasko (p. 62).

TINY MOUSE GOES TRAVELING

One fine spring morning Tiny Mouse decided to go traveling.
He made a boat from a tiny nutshell.
He made a paddle from a little spoon.
And he set out, paddling downstream.
As he paddled
Tiny Mouse sang a paddling song.

    "A nutshell for my boat! Wa . . . wa . . . wa . . .
    A spoon for my paddle! Ay . . . ay . . . ay. . . ."

Some children saw Tiny Mouse coming down the stream.
    "Let's tease Tiny Mouse!" they said.
And they began to call to him.
    "Tiny Mouse! Tiny Mouse!

Come over HERE! Come over HERE!"
Tiny Mouse stopped paddling.
     "What do you want?"
     "We have FOOD to eat!" called the children.

Now Tiny Mouse was known to be a glutton.
He had SUCH a big appetite.
     "What kind of food?"
     "We have BEAR meat."

     "YUK! YUK!
     TOO LARGE!
     I am a TINY Mouse!"

And Tiny Mouse paddled on downstream.
     "A nutshell for my boat! Wa . . . wa . . . wa . . .
     A spoon for my paddle! Ay . . . ay . . . ay . . ."

Children on the other side of the river saw him coming.
     "Tiny Mouse! Tiny Mouse!
     Come over HERE! Come over HERE!"
     "What do you want?"
     "We have FOOD!"

     "What kind of food?"
     "We have DEER meat."

     "YUK! YUK!
     TOO LARGE!
     I am a TINY mouse!"

Tiny Mouse paddled on downstream.
"A nutshell for my boat! Wa . . . wa . . . wa . . .
A spoon for my paddle! Ay . . . ay . . . ay. . . . !"

The children of the next village saw him coming.
"Tiny Mouse! Tiny Mouse!
Come over HERE! Come over HERE!"
"Why should I come?"
"We have something GOOD to eat."

"What do you have?"
"We have MOOSE!"

"YUK! YUK!
TOO BIG
I am a TINY mouse!"

Tiny Mouse paddled on downstream.
"A nutshell for my boat! Wa . . . wa . . . wa . . .
A spoon for my paddle! Ay . . . ay . . . ay . . ."

On the other side of the river,
children saw him coming.
"Tiny Mouse! Tiny Mouse!
Come over HERE! Come over HERE!"
"Why should I come?"
"We have FOOD to eat."

"What kind of food?"
"We have. . . . CARIBOU!"

"YUK! YUK!
TOO BIG!
I am a TINY mouse!"

Tiny mouse paddled on downstream.
      "A nutshell for my boat! Wa . . . wa . . . wa . . .
      A spoon for my paddle! Ay . . . ay . . . ay . . ."

THERE was an island right in the middle of the river!
On the island, children were calling.
      "Tiny Mouse! Tiny Mouse!
      Come over HERE! Come over HERE!"
      "Why should I come?"
      "We have FOOD to eat."

      "What kind of food?"
      "We have SALMON EGGS!"

      "SALMON EGGS!
      Are they TINY?"

      "Yes.
      They are VERY tiny."

      "Well, so am I!
      Here I COME!"

Tiny Mouse beached his little boat.
He grabbed his spoon-paddle.
He ran up the beach.

Tiny Mouse dug his spoon paddle right into those salmon eggs
and began to stuff himself.

> "Glub . . . glub . . . glub . . .
> GOOD!
> Glub . . . glub . . . glub . . .
> GOOD! GOOD!
> Glub . . . glub . . . glub . . .
> GOOD! GOOD! GOOD!"

Tiny Mouse stuffed himself until his little tummy stuck out.
His tummy got rounder and rounder and rounder. . . .
Such a glutton, that Tiny Mouse.

> "Let's tease Tiny Mouse," said the children.
> "Tiny Mouse! Tiny Mouse!" they called.
> "Your little boat is floating away!"

> "Eeek! Eeek! My nutshell BOAT!"

Tiny Mouse leaped up so fast that he fell right over onto his tummy.
His fat little tummy POPPED open!
And out spilled all of the salmon eggs he had been stuffing
    into himself.

> "Eeek! Eeek! My dinner is LOST!" wailed Tiny Mouse.
> "Quick, children. Bring me a needle and a wax thread."

The children ran to their mother for a needle and thread.
Tiny Mouse sewed his poor tummy back together again.

Then a very sad Tiny Mouse climbed into his little nutshell boat and
    drifted off downstream.

He was so sad that he couldn't even sing his paddling song.
He just sat in his little boat and moped.

So his little nutshell boat sang for him
        "A nutshell for a boat! Wa . . . wa . . . wa . . .
        A spoon for a paddle! Ay . . . ay . . . ay . . ."

And that's the story of Tiny Mouse who was SUCH a glutton.

NOTES ON TELLING

It can be fun to let the audience suggest the food each group of children offer Tiny Mouse. Let the story become playful—if the group want to offer him hippopotamus, that is all right. You may add as many wayside stops to the story as you like, just end with the tiny salmon eggs. The children who call to Tiny Mouse should be giggling as they offer him such large food, since they know he can't eat it.

    After telling the story, you may want to let the children act it out. There are plenty of parts here for a number of children, or the same children can run from side to side of the stream, teasing Tiny Mouse repeatedly as he floats along.

    I made up a tune to go with his paddling song.

COMPARATIVE NOTES

A brief version of this Khanti tale is found in *Northern Lights: Fairly Tales of the Peoples of the North*, compiled by E. Pomerantseva, and translated by Irina Zheleznova (p. 48–

49). The children in that tale offer him pike, duck, and sturgeon roe. The "too large" element is my own addition to the tale.

Tales of gluttons appear under Motif W125.2 *Gluttony,* but this tale is more closely related to Z33.2 *The fat cat,* a motif in which a glutton eats everything in sight, is cut open from within or bursts, then sews its tummy up again.

THE SINGING TURTLE

Once there was a kind old man.
Right next door lived a mean old man.
Now, the kind old man was poor.
But the mean old man was rich.

One day as the kind old man was walking on the road,
he found a little turtle lying on its back.
Some cruel children had turned the turtle over
and it could not get back onto its feet again.
This is one thing a turtle cannot do for itself.

The kind old man picked up the little turtle,
turned it over gently,
and set it back onto its feet.

The little turtle lifted its head,
bowed to the kind old man,
and began to speak!

       "Thank you, kind sir.
       I would like to repay you for this kindness.
       It is possible I might make your fortune.
       I am a singing turtle."

The old man was astonished.
       "What? A turtle that can speak?
       And a singing turtle as well?"

       "Pick me up and I will sing for you."

The old man lifted the tiny turtle to his palm.
The turtle stretched out its little neck
and it began to sing.
       "Pyo . . . pyo . . . pyo . . .
       pyo . . . pyo . . . pyo . . .
       I'm a turtle
       pyo . . . pyo . . . pyo . . ."

       "You really can sing!
       And very well too!" said the kind old man.

       "I know many songs," said the turtle.
       "That was just my turtle song.
       Would you like to hear my mouse song?"

The little turtle stretched out his neck
    and began to sing again.
        "Squeak . . . squeak . . . squeak . . .
        squeak . . . squeak . . . squeak . . .
        I sing like a mouse
        squeak . . . squeak . . . squeak . . ."

        "I have many songs.
        What else would you like to hear?
        My cow song. . . ?
        My horse song. . . ?"

The old man saw at once that this singing turtle could bring him
    fortune.
He carried the turtle to the village and called the people to come and
    listen.
        "See what I have here!
        It is a singing turtle!"
He held out his hand,
set the little turtle on his palm,
and at once it began to sing its turtle song.
        "Pyo . . . pyo . . . pyo . . .
        pyo . . . pyo . . . pyo . . .
        I'm a turtle
        pyo . . . pyo . . . pyo . . ."

        "How wonderful!"
The people applauded.
        "Sing some more!"

"What would you like to hear?
My donkey song?
Bray . . . bray . . . bray . . .
bray . . . bray . . . bray . . .
I sing like a donkey
bray . . . bray . . . bray . . ."

People excitedly began to call out requests for songs.
"Sing the elephant song!"
"Can you sing a cat song?"
"Sing a crocodile song!"
The little turtle sang and sang.

When he had finished, the villagers filled the kind old man's hands with
coins.
"Thank you for bringing this little turtle to sing for us.
Please bring it back another day."

The kind old man took the turtle home to live with him.
Every day they went to a different village.
The turtle sang.
People piled coins in the old man's hands.
Soon he was no longer poor.
He had a fine silk comforter to sleep under.
He had fish to go with his rice every day.
And in the corner of his room he made a little bed for his friend, the
turtle.

In the evenings, after they had gone to bed,
the turtle would sing the kind old man to sleep.

"Pyo . . . pyo . . . pyo . . .
pyo . . . pyo . . . pyo . . .
go to sleep . . .
kind old man."

One day the mean old man next door heard about the singing turtle.
"All those coins should be MINE," he thought.
"Why should the poor man have such wealth.
He doesn't even know what to do with it."
And that night while the kind old man slept,
the mean old man crept into his room,
picked up the little turtle,
and hiding it inside his kimono,
tiptoed back to his own house.

The next day, the mean old rich man took the little turtle to the village.
"Everyone gather around!
I have a SINGING turtle!
Pay me your coins and I will make it sing."
They curiously handed over a few coins.
The mean old man held up the turtle for all to see.
"Now SING!
SING for these people.
Come on.
We're WAIT . . . ing."
But the little turtle would not.
It pulled in its front feet.
It pulled in its back feet.
It pulled in its tail.
It pulled in its head.
And SNAP . . . its shell closed fast.

No matter how the mean old man coaxed or threatened,
the little turtle would not come out.

"Fake!" shouted the crowd.
"Fake!"
They threw rotten fruit at the mean old man.
Then they went away.

The mean old man was furious.
He ran right back to the poor old man's house.
"Here is your 'singing' turtle!" he called out.
"It doesn't sing a note!"
And he THREW the little turtle against the side of the poor man's
house.

The turtle's shell smashed against the side of the house.
It fell to the earth.
The little shell was cracked.
The little head hung out.
The little turtle was dead.

Out ran the kind old man.
"What have you done?"
He picked up the little turtle and cradled it in his hands.
Quietly he scooped a hole in the ground.
Carefully he laid the turtle in the hole.
Gently he covered the turtle over with earth.
He sat by the tiny mound
and his tears fell drop by drop onto the little turtle's grave.

As his tears fell on the grave,
something remarkable happened.
A tiny green shoot began to grow from the grave.
A tiny bamboo shoot.
Growing and growing,
it pointed toward the sky.
Higher and higher it grew.
Its tip disappeared into the clouds.

And then,
while the old man stood staring up in amazement,
something began to come down the bamboo shoot.
Something small and green,
coming closer and closer,
until he saw that . . .
it was a tiny TURTLE!

And behind it came another turtle.
And behind that another.
And another . . . and . . .
There were HUNDREDS of tiny green turtles,
all running down the bamboo shoot toward the kind old man!

When the first little turtle reached the kind old man,
it stopped.
It opened its little mouth.
And PLOP!
Out fell a golden coin,
right into the old man's hand.

Then it turned and ran back up the bamboo shoot,
waggling its little tail.
The second turtle reached the kind old man.
It opened its little mouth . . .
    PLOP!
Out fell another golden coin.

Down came the turtles.
One by one they stopped,
opened their little mouths,
and . . .
    PLOP!
Dropped their golden coins for the kind old man.

Soon he was surrounded by a mound of golden coins.
He would never be poor again.

But the mean old man next door saw what was going on.
He ran to the bamboo shoot and pushed the kind old man out of the
    way.
        "Move aside old man.
        These golden coins should be MINE."
And he held his hands up greedily to catch the turtles' coins.
When the next little turtle saw that it was the MEAN old man standing
    there,
it stopped.
It opened its little mouth . . .
        "Nah . . . nah-nah . . . nah . . . nah!"
It stuck out its tongue at the mean old man!
Then it turned and ran back up the bamboo shoot.

One by one the tiny turtles ran down the bamboo shoot.
Each stuck out its tongue at the mean old man,
        "Nah . . . nah-nah . . . nah . . . nah!",
then ran back up the bamboo shoot
and disappeared into the clouds.

That is the story of the kind old man
and the mean old man
and their rewards.

NOTES ON TELLING

None of my sources included music for the turtle's song, so I invented one. Use my tune or invent your own. The children will want to sing with you, and they might like to tell you what each animal's voice should sound like. I ask them what animal's song they want the turtle to sing next, and often we play at inventing songs for several animals during the story's telling.

Pyo, pyo, pyo, pyo, pyo, pyo.

I sing like a tur - tle. Pyo, pyo, pyo.

COMPARATIVE NOTES

This is a good tale to use for classroom discussion of folktale variants, since several interesting variations are available in juvenile folktale collections. This tale is motif 210.2 *Talking animal or object refuses to talk on demand. Discoverer is unable to prove his claim: is beaten.* Harold Courlander and George Herzog's *The Cow-Tail Switch and Other West African Stories* (p. 65) includes a variant from Ghana in which a tortoise plays a sansa (thumb piano) and sings. Philippe Thoby-Marcelin and Pierre Marcelin include a similar tale in their *The Singing Turtle and Other Tales from Haiti* (p. 21). Harold Courlander includes another Haitian version in his *The Piece of Fire, and Other Haitian Tales* (p. 29), in which the sassy turtle sticks his head out of the water and sings after his escape. Only in the Japanese variant does the turtle perform for a kind person with whom it bonds. Other variants feature only the unkind individual who tries to capitalize on the singing animal and is tricked.

Japanese variants may be found in *Japanese Children's Stories* by Florence Sakade (p. 93) and in *Hold Tight, Stick Tight: A Collection of Japanese Folktales* by Elizabeth Scofield (p. 9).

An African variant which has been transplanted to America is the "Talking Skull" in which a skull found lying in the road says, "My big mouth brought me here and yours will do the same." When the man brags of finding a talking skull, he is beheaded for lying. The skull says, "I told you your big mouth would do the same." African-American variants can be found in Maria Leach's, *The Thing at the Foot of the Bed and Other Scary Tales* (p. 49) and Harold Courlander's *Terrapin's Pot of Sense* (p. 74). A Nupe variant is found in Leo Frobenius and Douglas C. Fox's, *African Genesis* (p. 161) and a variant from the Congo is in Phyllis Savory's *Congo Fireside Tales*. Savory's version is reprinted in Freya Littledale's, *Ghosts and Spirits of Many Lands* (p. 67).

From Burma comes the tale of the beheaded head that tells a servant to fetch the king. The head remains silent and the servant is beheaded. The head now laughs. It is buried and a cocoanut grows from the head. When you shake the cocoanut, you can hear the head still gurgling with laughter. This tale is in Maung Htin Aung and Helen Trager's *A Kingdom Lost for a Drop of Honey and Other Burmese Folktales* (p. 43). The tale includes Motif F54.2 *Plant grows to sky* and J2415 *Foolish imitation of lucky man.*

THE TEENY WEENY BOP

Once there was a little old girl called the Teeny Weeny Bop.
She lived all by herself and she was lonely.
One morning the Teeny Weeny Bop got up and started sweeping her floor.
She was sweeping her floor . . .
And sweeping her floor . . .
And sweeping her floor . . .
And. . . .

She found a SILVER COIN on the floor!
"My LUCK is MADE!" said the Teeny Weeny Bop.
"I'll go right to town and buy myself a pet.
Then I won't be alone anymore.
Think I'll buy myself a fat little PIG!"
And she started off down the road.

"TO MARKET, TO MARKET, TO BUY A FAT PIG!
HOME AGAIN, HOME AGAIN, JIGGETY-JIG!"

She got to the town and went right to the pig farmer.
"Mr. Pig Farmer, I have a silver coin. Could I buy a PIG?"
"You sure can. Here's a fat little pig, just for you."

She put the pig under her arm and started back home.
"I WENT TO MARKET, AND I BOUGHT A FAT PIG.
NOW I'M COMING HOME AGAIN, JIGGETY-JIG!"

When she got home, she put that little pig out in her garden, and she
locked the garden gate.
"You'll be safe there, little pig.

She sat down in her chair, and she rocked, and she sang.
"I went to market, and I bought a fat pig.
Then I came home again, Jiggety-Jig."
She went to bed.
She went to sleep.
And she slept real sound.

In the morning the Teeny Weeny Bop got up and went out to check her
little pig.
"Oh, NO!"
What do you think that little pig had done during the night,
while she was sleeping so sound?

He had eaten up all her beans and her tomatoes.
He had rooted out all of her carrots and potatoes.
And he had made a big mud wallow right in the middle of her garden!

The Teeny Weeny Bop said,
>"PIG, PIG, WHAT A MESS YOU'VE MADE!
>I'M TAKING YOU TO MARKET AND I'M GOING TO
>TRADE!"

She thought she would trade that pig for a nice little CAT.
>"TO MARKET, TO MARKET, TO BUY A FAT CAT.
>HOME AGAIN, HOME AGAIN, JIGGETY-JAT."

She went to the cat lady.
>"Ma'am, would you trade me a cat for this pig?"
>"Sure. Here's a nice little cat for you."

Back home she went.
>"I WENT TO MARKET, AND I BOUGHT A FAT CAT.
>NOW I'M COMING HOME AGAIN, JIGGETY-JAT.

>"I won't put this cat in the garden.
>I don't want another mess.
>I'll keep my cat right here . . . in the LIVING ROOM."

She sat down in her chair, and she rocked, and she sang.
>"I went to market, and I bought a fat cat.
>Then I came home again, Jiggety-Jat."

She went to bed.
She went to sleep.
And she slept real sound.

In the morning, the Teeny Weeny Bop got up and checked on her cat.
>"Oh, NO!"

What do you think that cat had done while she was sleeping so sound?

It had scratched up all the furniture.
It had ripped up the curtains.
It had knocked the lamp over and broken it.
It had made a mess of the entire living room.

She said,
> "CAT, CAT, WHAT A MESS YOU'VE MADE!
> I'M TAKING YOU TO MARKET AND I'M GOING TO
> TRADE!"

She said, "I think I'll get a little HAMSTER."
> "TO MARKET, TO MARKET, TO BUY A FAT HAMSTER.
> HOME AGAIN, HOME AGAIN, JIGGETY-JAMSTER.

> "Hamster seller, would you trade me a hamster for my cat?"
> "Sure. Here's a fat little hamster for you."

Back home she went.
> "I WENT TO MARKET, AND I BOUGHT A FAT
> HAMSTER.
> NOW I'M COMING HOME AGAIN, JIGGETY-JAMSTER.

> "I don't want to have any more trouble with this pet.
> I'm going to keep it safe.
> I'll put it in the KITCHEN CUPBOARD!"

She sat down in her chair, she rocked, and she sang.
> "I went to market, and I bought a fat hamster.
> Then I came home again, Jiggety-Jamster."
She went to bed.
She went to sleep.
And she slept real sound.

150

In the morning she got up and checked on her little pet.

"Oh, NO!"

What do you think that little hamster had done, while she was sleeping so sound?

It had eaten up all the cereal in the cupboard.

It had knocked over all the glasses and broke them.

It had chewed holes in the walls of the cupboard.

It had made a mess of everything.

She said,

"HAMSTER, HAMSTER, WHAT A MESS YOU'VE MADE!

I'M TAKING YOU TO MARKET AND I'M GOING TO TRADE!"

She said,

"I think I'll buy myself a tiny pet, that won't make any trouble at all.

I'll buy myself a fat little ANT."

"TO MARKET, TO MARKET, TO BUY A FAT ANT.

HOME AGAIN, HOME AGAIN, JIGGETY-JANT."

"Ant seller, would you trade me a fat little ant for my hamster?"

"Sure, I would. Here's your fat little ant."

Back home she went.

"I WENT TO MARKET, AND I BOUGHT A FAT ANT.

THEN I CAME HOME AGAIN JIGGETY-JANT.

"I'm not going to let this ant make any trouble.

I'll keep it in a safe place.

Maybe in a jar.
I know. I'll keep it in my COOKY JAR."

She sat in her chair, she rocked, and she sang.
"I went to market, and I bought a fat ant.
Then I came home again, Jiggety-Jant."
She went to bed.
She went to sleep.
And she slept real sound.

In the morning she got up and checked on her little pet.
"Oh, NO!"
What do you think that little ant had done while she slept so sound?

It ate all the chocolate chips out of her cookies!
It made holes in everything.
It left nothing but a pile of crumbs and was starting to eat those!
She said,
"ANT, ANT, WHAT A MESS YOU'VE MADE!
I'M TAKING YOU TO MARKET AND I'M GOING TO
TRADE!"

Then she said, "NO,
I've had enough of these pets.
I don't like the ant,
I don't like the hamster,
I don't like the cat.
I think I'd rather have a fat little pig like I had in the first
place."
So she went back to the market.

152

"TO MARKET, TO MARKET, TO BUY A FAT PIG.
HOME AGAIN, HOME AGAIN, JIGGETY-JIG.

"Pig farmer, would you trade me a fat pig for my ant?"
But the pig farmer would not.

"Well then, I'll trade back for a cat.

"Cat seller, would you trade me a cat for my ant?"
But the cat seller would not.

"Well then, I'll just trade for a hamster."

"Hamster seller, would you trade a hamster for my ant?"
But the hamster seller would not.

"Well then I'll trade my ant back for a silver coin."

"Ant seller, would you give me a silver coin for my ant?"
But the ant seller just laughed at her.

"I started with a silver coin.
Then I had a fat pig.
I had a fat cat.
I had a fat hamster.
Now all I have is a little ant.
And no one will trade.
I guess I've traded my luck out."
She turned the little ant loose
and she went back home, so sad.

She got her broom and started sweeping her house.
Sweeping her house . . .
and sweeping her house . . .
and sweeping her house . . .
and sweeping her house . . .
and sweeping her house . . .
and sweeping her house . . .
and. . . .
    She found a SILVER COIN!

        "MY LUCK IS MADE!
        I'll go to town and buy myself a PET!
        Think I'll buy a fat little HOG!

        "TO MARKET, TO MARKET, TO BUY A FAT HOG
        HOME AGAIN HOME AGAIN JIGGETY-JOG."

NO MORE, NO MORE, TEENY WEENY BOP,
THIS CRAZY STORY HAS GOT TO *STOP!*

NOTES ON TELLING

Pacing is important in this story. The chants should be rhythmical. Slap legs or snap fingers as you chant,

        "To market, to market, to buy a fat pig.
        Home again, home again, jiggety-jig"

The trip to and from town is jaunty and full of energy. Once home, The Teeny Weeny Bop sits in her chair and rocks sleepily back and forth, clapping quietly or snapping her fingers as she chants. This is soporific in effect. Then a sudden break:

> "She went to bed.
> She went to sleep.
> And she slept real sound!"

Then with "And in the morning. . . ," the pace picks up and the whole thing starts over again.

The audience will join you on the chants, of course. Clapping or leg-slapping works best for young children, but finger-snapping seems cooler to older groups. Though I have given a text here for the entire tale, the tale's elements will be created by the audience during each telling.

Let the audience suggest what animal Teeny Weeny Bop might buy next. Point out that no one would trade her a BIGGER animal, so it must be smaller each time. I ask the audience what animal she could buy, and take suggestions until I get the one I like best. "Dog? . . . That would work. Horse? . . . Too big—no one would trade her a horse for a pig. Cat? . . . Yes! Let's have her buy a cat!"

A cat works well because the audience will be able to think of lots of things it can do to make a mess in the living room. Somebody will always suggest a cat if you hold out for suggestions long enough. But be prepared to ad lib if you get stuck with a turtle, parrot, or other exotic pet. After all, the audience is in charge and it is best to stick to your ground rules. Usually, though, it is possible to elicit the animal you want with a little trickery.

While it is often easy to evoke suggestions of a hamster, gerbil, or mouse to fit nicely into the cupboard for the third episode, the last animal is a little more difficult. An ant can be put in the cookie jar. I ask "Where shall I put it?" and someone eventually says, "in a jar." Then I say, "Oh, I'll put it in my COOKIE jar!" However, my favorite last animal is a slug. I can sometimes draw "slug" from the audience by asking for smaller animals; and saying "like a snail" can put "slug" in someone's mind. The slug can be put in the refrigerator. It slimes everything, eats up the lettuce, etc. (Seattle kids usually suggest that it drinks up all the beer, too, because we put bowls of beer in our yards to kill the slugs here. It is said that slugs crawl in and drown.)

This story is definitely not for the timid. You must be prepared to let the group play with you, and if they force an unwanted pet into the story, it's up to you to figure out what to do with it!

155

You can end the tale briefly by explaining that she could not trade back for the pig, or you can play with the ending by approaching audience members as if they were the cat seller, pig seller, etc., and try to get them to trade with you. Ask why they won't trade you a pig for your slug. "It's too small," they may answer, "It's not worth a pig."

Teeny Weeny Bop's last sweeping episode begins dejectedly building slowly to an excited frenzy as she recovers from her depression and . . . finds another coin!

COMPARATIVE NOTES

This tale was created from a much briefer story included by Australian teller Jean Chapman in her *Tell Me Another Tale: Stories, Verses, Songs and Things to Do* (p. 20–21). This delightful book turned up in our library book sale! (My thanks to whomever ferried it over to the U.S.) The other tales in Chapman's collection are familiar folktales, and this certainly has the feel of a folktale to it, but as yet I haven't located other variants. Chapman's much shorter version starts with five geese to fatten for Christmas. She sells them for four pennies and buys a pig, sells it for four pennies and buys a hen, sells it for two pennies and buys a cat, which runs away. . . . Then she finds another silver coin. The chanting bits and the increasingly smaller animals are my addition—actually, mine and that of the many children of Bothell, Washington, who listened and added their bits to the tellings. The tale, as I tell it, is related to Motif J2081.1 *Foolish bargain: horse for cow, cow for hog, etc. Finally nothing left.* (Type 1415) and to Z41.5 *Lending and repaying: progressively worse (or better) bargain.* (Type 2034).

A PENNY AND A HALF

I once had a penny and a half.

With my penny and a half I bought a hen.
Ay! Ay! What a hen!
My little hen . . . gave me an egg.
I had a hen. I had an egg.
And I still had my penny and a half.

I once had a penny and a half.
With my penny and a half I bought a duck.
Ay! Ay! What a duck!
My little duck . . . gave me a duckling.
I had a duck. I had a duckling.
I had a hen. I had an egg.
And I still had my penny and a half.

I once had a penny and a half.
With my penny and a half I bought a cat.
Ay! Ay! What a cat!
My little cat . . . gave me a kitten.
I had a cat. I had a kitten.
I had a duck. I had a duckling.
I had a hen. I had an egg.
And I still had my penny and a half.

I once had a penny and a half.
With my penny and a half I bought a pig.
Ay! Ay! What a pig!
My little pig . . . gave me a piglet.
I had a pig. I had a piglet.
I had a cat. I had a kitten.
I had a duck. I had a duckling.
I had a hen. I had an egg.
And I still had my penny and a half.

I once had a penny and a half.
With my penny and a half I bought a cow.
Ay! Ay! What a cow!

My little cow . . . gave me a calf.
I had a cow. I had a calf.
I had a pig. I had a piglet.
I had a cat. I had a kitten.
I had a duck. I had a duckling.
I had a hen. I had an egg.
And I still had my penny and a half.

I once had a penny and a half.
With my penny and a half I bought a horse.
Ay! Ay! What a horse!
My little horse . . . gave me a colt.
I had a horse. I had a colt.
I had a cow. I had a calf.
I had a pig. I had a piglet.
I had a cat. I had a kitten.
I had a duck. I had a duckling.
I had a hen. I had an egg.
And I still had my penny and a half.

I once had a penny and a half.
With my penny and a half I bought a *guitar*.
Ay! Ay! What a guitar!
Every time I played that guitar . . .
The horse danced, and the colt danced.
The cow danced, and the calf danced.
The pig danced, and the piglet danced.
The duck danced, and the duckling danced.
The cat danced, and the kitten danced.
The hen danced, and the egg danced too!

And I still have my penny and a half!
Ay! Ay! What a penny and a half!

NOTES ON TELLING

The audience will want to join in on your final teasing line at each refrain: "And I still have a penny and a half!" It would be fun to pretend paying an audience member for each animal with a real coin. Palm the coin, and produce it gleefully again to show on each teasing line.

For even more fun with this tale, encourage the audience members to suggest animals to buy at each refrain. I start with a hen and egg and I ask the audience to gradually suggest ever larger animals. Older children often end with a dinosaur and dinosaurlet dancing with hippos, horses, etc. With preschool children, the tale may become more of a recounting of farm animals and their babies.

COMPARATIVE NOTES

Retold from *Folklore Chileno* by Oreste Plath (p. 268–270). The complete list in the Spanish version is:

Yo tenía mi real y medio.
Con mi real y medio compré una gringa,
    ay qué gringa,
y la gringa me dio un gringuito.
Yo tengo la gringa, yo tengo el gringuito,
yo tengo la lora, yo tengo el lorito,
yo tengo la cabra, yo tengo el cabrito,
yo tengo la mona, yo tengo el monito,
yo tengo la burra, yo tengo el burrito,
yo tengo la vaca, yo tengo el ternero,
yo tengo la polla, yo tengo los huevos,
y siempre me quedo con mi real y medio.

I altered the text in my English version, in order to keep the play on sounds of the diminutives (duck, ducklings). A straight translation (monkey, little monkey) sounded

160

clunky. Also, I wanted to keep something of the rhythm of the Chilean text. However, English cannot match the Spanish "bailaba la cabra, bailaba el cabrito, bailaba la mona, bailaba el monito."

A Mexican variant appears in *Folktales of Mexico* by Americo Paredes as "La Chiva (The Nanny Goat)." That tale lacks the guitar ending of the Chilean version. Musical notation is given for the Paredes tale, but as the Spanish text is lacking there are not words to fit to the music. It was collected in Matamoros, Tamulipas in 1954. Paredes considers the tale related to Motif Z22 *Ehod mi yodea (One: who knows?)* (Type 2010) and Z23 *How the rich man paid his servant,* (in which a farmer pays his servant in the first year with a hen, in the second with a cock, in the third with a goose, the fourth with a goat, the fifth with a cow, the sixth with a horse, the seventh with a girl, then finally with the farmstead). He compares it also to "The Song of the Kid" in the Jewish Passover tradition.

This is a cumulative tale (Z20), though Plath includes it in a chapter of endless tales (Z11).

Part II: Suggested Uses and Sources

SUGGESTED AGE/GRADE FOR TELLING

TALE	3	4	K	1	2	3	4	5	6	JH	HS	Adult
Kanji-Jo, the Nestlings	X	X	X	X	X	X						
A Penny and a Half	X	X	X	X	X	X	X					
The Snow Bunting's Lullaby	X	X	X	X	X	X	X					
Please All . . . Please None	X	X	X	X	X	X	X					
Tiny Mouse Goes Traveling	X	X	X	X	X	X	X					
Why Koala Has No Tail	X	X	X	X	X	X	X					
The Strawberries of the Little Men	X	X	X	X	X	X	X					
Biyera Well	X	X	X	X	X	X	X					
The Singing Turtle	X	X	X	X	X	X	X	X				
The Teeny Weeny Bop	X	X	X	X	X	X	X	X	X			
Turkey Girl	X	X	X	X	X	X	X	X	X			
Grandfather Bear is Hungry	X	X	X	X	X	X	X	X	X			
The Elk and the Wren	X	X	X	X	X	X	X	X	X	X	X	X
Look Back and See	X	X	X	X	X	X	X	X	X	X	X	X
Little Cricket's Marriage: Ms. Cricket takes a Husband	X	X	X	X	X	X	X	X	X	X	X	X
Ms. Cricket Does Her Laundry			X	X	X	X	X	X	X	X	X	X
Katchi Katchi Blue Jay			X	X	X	X	X	X	X			
Domingo Siete					X	X	X	X	X			
Two Women Hunt for Ground Squirrels					X	X	X	X	X	X	X	X
Quail Song						X	X	X	X	X	X	X
Bear-Child							X	X	X	X	X	X

WHOLE LANGUAGE USES

Rhythm/Rhyme

Domingo Siete

Kanji-Jo, the Nestlings

Turkey Girl

Look Back and See

The Snow Bunting's Lullaby

Biyera Well

A Penny and a Half

The Bear-Child

Tiny Mouse Goes Traveling

Ms. Cricket Does Her Laundry

The Teeny Weeny Bop

Two Women Hunt for Ground Squirrels

Simile

Look Back and See

Sequencing

Smaller to Larger

A Penny and a Half

The Teeny Weeny Bop

The Bear-Child

Combining

Please All . . . Please None

Matching (Like-Unlike)

Tiny Mouse Goes Traveling (appropriate size for food)

Ms. Cricket Takes a Husband (appropriate size for mate)

Kanji-jo, the Nestlings (appropriate size, color, and shape for mother)

Math/Economics

The Teeny Weeny Bop (bad trades)

A Penny and a Half (cumulative reproductive nonsense)

Music

Domingo Siete

Kanji-jo, the Nestlings

Turkey Girl

Look Back and See

The Snow Bunting's Lullaby

Tiny Mouse Goes Traveling

The Teeny Weeny Bop

Quail Song

The Singing Turtle

The Elk and the Wren

Dance

Domingo Siete

Kanji-Jo, the Nestlings

Turkey Girl

Look Back and See

The Teeny Weeny Bop

A Penny and a Half

167

Creative Drama

Biyera Well

Domingo Siete

Kanji-Jo, the Nestlings

Tiny Mouse Goes Traveling

Turkey Girl

Grandfather Bear is Hungry

Many of the tales lend themselves to dramatic re-enactment, but these are especially useful for group creative drama replay.

Science

Tales Explaining Animal Nature

Katchi Katchi Blue Jay (why blue jay has top-knot,
     why blue jay has raspy voice)

Quail Song (quail's song)

Grandfather Bear is Hungry (origin of chipmunk's stripes)

Turkey Girl (why wild turkeys live on mesas)

Why Koala Has No Tail (why koala has no tail)

Other Tales Showing Animal Behavior

Kanji-jo, the Nestlings (bushfowl, dove, hummingbird)

Snow Bunting's Lullaby (snow bunting, raven)

The Elk and the Wren (wren, elk)

The Bear Child (polar bear)

Why Koala Has No Tail (koala, tree kangaroo)

Ecology

Two Women Hunt for Ground Squirrels (taboo on hunting young of the species)

Gardening

Biyera Well
The Strawberries of the Little Men

CULTURAL AREAS

Africa

   Mende   Kanji-jo, the Nestlings

   Tanzania/Haya   Look Back and See

Asia

   Japan   The Singing Turtle

Australia

                      The Teeny Weeny Bop

   Aborigine   Why Koala Has No Tail

Europe

   England   The Strawberries of the Little Men

   U.S.S.R./Eiven   Grandfather Bear Is Hungry

   U.S.S.R./Khanti   Tiny Mouse Goes Traveling

   U.S.S.R./Siberia   The Snow Bunting's Lullaby

Latin America

   Argentina   Domingo Siete

   Chile   A Penny and a Half

Middle East

   Egypt   The Biyera Well

   Palestinian Arab   Little Cricket's Marriage

Native American

   Cahuilla   Quail Song

   Inuit, Baffin Island   Bear-Child

   Makah   The Elk and the Wren

   Nisqually   Katchi Katchi Blue Jay

   Tanaiana Athabaskan   Two Women Hunt for Ground Squirrels

   Zuñi   Turkey Girl

CHARACTER TRAITS EXEMPLIFIED IN THESE TALES

Positive Traits

GENEROSITY

Grandfather Bear Is Hungry

GENTLE MALE

Grandfather Bear Is Hungry
The Snow Bunting's Lullaby

KINDNESS

Grandfather Bear Is Hungry
The Singing Turtle

POLITENESS (Saying Thank You)

The Strawberries of the Little Men

MARRYING A SUITABLE MATE

Little Cricket's Marriage

MODERATION (Knowing when to say "Enough")

The Strawberries of the Little Men

PARENTING (Caring parents)

Kanji-Jo, the Nestlings
The Snow Bunting's Lullaby

STEADFASTNESS

Look Back and See

STRONG FEMALE

The Elk and the Wren
Little Cricket's Marriage

Unsuitable Character Traits

ADVICE, IGNORING

Katchi Katchi Blue Jay

THINKING FOR ONESELF, FAILURE TO DO SO

Please All . . . Please None

UNDERSTANDING, LACK OF

The Bear-Child

UNKINDNESS

Domingo Siete
The Singing Turtle
The Strawberries of the Little Men
Two Women Hunt for Ground Squirrels

STRONG WOMEN AND GENTLE MEN

Though it was not the intention of this collection to seek such tales, a note on those included may be useful. In "The Snow Bunting's Lullaby" it is Papa Snow Bunting who sings the lullaby which calms their crying chick. It was this gentle-father image which especially attracted me to the tale. "Grandfather Bear is Hungry" shows Bear in a gentle light, as a super-strong male gently strokes a tiny chipmunk in gratitude. "Two Women Hunt for Ground Squirrels," "The Teeny Weeny Bop," and "Turkey Girl" all have women protagonists, but it is the sassy Ms. Cricket of "Ms. Cricket Takes a Husband" who shows role reversal, as she sets out to court a mate for herself.

BIBLIOGRAPHY OF WORKS CONSULTED

Aarne, Antti and Stith Thompson. *The Types of the Folktale: A Classification and Bibliography.* Folklore Fellows Communications, no. 184. Helsinki: Suomalainen Tiedeakatemia, 1973.

Ammar, Hamed. *Growing Up in an Egyptian Village: Silwa, Province of Aswan.* London: Routledge & Kegan Paul Ltd., n.d.; New York: Octagon, 1966.

Belpré, Pura. *Perez and Martina.* New York: Warne, 1932.

Berson, Harry. *Turkey Girl.* New York: Macmillan, 1983.

Briggs, Katharine M. *A Dictionary of British Folk-Tales.* Part A, vol. 1. Bloomington: Indiana University Press, 1970.

Bushnaq, Inea. *Arab Folktales.* New York: Pantheon, 1986.

Caswell, Helen. *Shadows from the Singing House.* Rutland, Vt.: Charles E. Tuttle, 1968.

Chapman, Jean. *Tell Me Another Tale: Stories, Verses, Songs and Things To Do.* Sydney: Hodder & Stoughton, 1976.

Cheney, Cora. *Tales from a Taiwanese Kitchen.* New York: Dodd, Mead, 1976.

Chertudi, Susana, ed. *Juan Soldao: Cuentos de Folklóricos de la Argentina.* Buenos Aires: Editorial Universitaria de Buenos Aires, 1962.

Colldén, Lisa. *Trésors de la Tradition Orale Sakata: Proverbes, Mythes, Légends, Fables, Chansons et Devinettes de Sakata.* Uppsala, Sweden: Almqvist och Wiksell International, 1979.

Courlander, Harold. *The Piece of Fire, and Other Haitian Tales.* New York: Harcourt, 1942.

Courlander, Harold. *Terrapin's Pot of Sense.* New York: Holt, 1957.

Courlander, Harold, and Ezekiel Eshugbayi. *Olode the Hunter.* New York: Harcourt, Brace & World, 1968.

Courlander, Harold, and George Herzog. *The Cow-Tail Switch and Other West African Stories.* New York: Holt, Rinehart and Winston, 1947.

Cushing, Frank Hamilton. *Zuñi Folktales.* New York: G. P. Putnam's Sons, 1901.

Dobie, J. Frank. *Tongues of the Monte.* New York: Little, Brown, & Co., 1947. Reprint. Austin: University of Texas Press, 1980.

Dorliae, Peter. *Animals Mourn For Da Leopard and Other West African Tales*. Indianapolis: Bobbs-Merrill, 1970.

Downing, Charles. *Tales of the Hodja*. New York: Walck, 1965.

El-Shamy, Hasan M. *Folktales of Egypt*. Chicago: University of Chicago Press, 1980.

The Father, the Son, and the Donkey. Seattle: Sign-a-Vision, 1986. Video cassette.

Fitzgerald, Burdette S. *World Tales for Creative Dramatics and Storytelling*. Englewood Cliffs, N.J.: Prentice-Hall, Inc., 1962.

Folke Eventyr Fra Sidir. Moscow: Malysh Publishers, 1976.

Frobenius, Leo, and Douglas C. Fox. *African Genesis*. New York: Benjamin Blom, 1937.

Fuja, Abayomi. *Fourteen Hundred Cowries and Other African Tales*. New York: Lothrop, Lee & Shepard, 1971.

Garf, Anna. *Life with Granny Kandiki: Based on Tales from the Soviet North*. Moscow: Progress Publishers, 1978.

Gilham, Charles. *Beyond the Clapping Mountains*. New York: MacMillan, 1943.

Haviland, Virginia. *North American Legends*. New York: Philomel, 1979.

Henry, Jeanette, and Rupert Costo. *A Thousand Years of American Indian Storytelling: A Weewish Tree Reader*. San Francisco: The Indian Historian Press, 1981.

Htin Aung, Maung, and Helen Trager. *A Kingdom Lost for a Drop of Honey and Other Burmese Folktales*. New York: Parents, 1968.

Jackson, Kenneth M. T. (Grey Eagle). *Let Us Honor That Rascal Raven*. Kauta Keino, Norway: DAT, O.S., 1991.

Jacottet, Edouard. *The Treasury of Ba-Suto Lore*. The Folktale Series. Reprint 1908 ed. (2 vols. in 1). New York: AMS Pr.

Jagendorf, Moritz. *King of the Mountain*. New York: Vanguard, 1960.

Leach, Maria. *The Thing at the Foot of the Bed and Other Scary Tales*. Cleveland: World, 1959.

Littledale, Freya. *Ghosts and Spirits of Many Lands*. Garden City: Doubleday, 1970.

MacDonald, Margaret Read. *The Storyteller's Sourcebook: a Subject, Title, and Motif Index to Children's Folklore Collections*. Detroit: Gale Research/Neal-Schuman, 1982.

———. *Twenty Tellable Tales: Audience Participation Folktales for the Beginning Storyteller*. New York: H. W. Wilson, 1986.

176

Matson, Emerson N. *Legends of the Great Chiefs*. Nashville: Thomas Nelson, 1972.

Millman, Lawrence. *A Kayak Full of Ghosts: Eskimo Tales*. Santa Barbara: Capra Press, 1987.

Muhawi, Ibrahim, and Sharif Kanaana. *Speak, Bird, Speak Again: Palestinian Arab Folktales*. Berkely: University of California Press, 1989.

Paredes, Americo. *Folktales of Mexico*. Chicago: University of Chicago Press, 1970.

Parsons, Elsie Clews. "Pueblo-Indian Folk-Tales, Probably of Spanish Provenience" in *Journal of American Folklore* 31, no. 120 (1918): 234–235.

Peterson, Helene. "Too Proud Elk" on *Songs and Stories from Neah Bay*. Canyon Records, 4143 North 16 Street, Phoenix, Arizona 85016 (1976).

Plath, Oreste. *Folkore Chileno*. Santiago: Nascimento, 1969.

Pomerantseva, E. *Northern Lights: Fairy Tales of the People of the North*. Translated by Irina Zheleznova. Moscow: Progress Publishers, 1976.

Reed, A. W. *Aboriginal Legends: Animal Tales*. French Forest, Australia: Reed Books Pty. Ltd., 1978, 1987.

Sakade, Florence. *Japanese Children's Stories*. Rutland, Vt.: Charles E. Tuttle, 1952.

Savory, Phyllis. *Congo Fireside Tales*. New York: Hastings House, 1962.

Scofield, Elizabeth. *Hold Tight, Stick Tight: A Collection of Japanese Folktales*. Palo Alto, Calif.: Kodansha, 1966.

Seitel, Peter. *See So That We May See: Performances and Interpretations of Traditional Tales from Tanzania*. Bloomington: Indiana University Press, 1980.

Sierra, Judy. *Fantastic Theater: Puppets and Plays for Young Performers and Young Audiences*. New York: H. W. Wilson, 1991.

Solasko, Fainna, trans. *Kutkha the Raven: Animal Stories of the North*. Moscow: Malysh Publishers, 1981.

Stephan, Stephan H. "Palestinian Animal Stories and Fables" in *Journal of the Palestine Oriental Society* III, no. 4 (1928):181.

Tenenbaum, Joan M., compiler. *Dena'ina Sukdu'a: Traditional Stories of the Tanaina Athabaskans*. Fairbanks: Alaska Native Language Center, University of Alaska, 1984.

Thoby-Marcelin, Philippe, and Pierre Marcelin. *The Singing Turtle and Other Tales From Haiti*. New York: Farrar, Straus & Giroux, 1971.

Thompson, Stith. *Motif-Index of Folk-Literature.* 6 vols. Bloomington: Indiana University Press, 1966.

———. *Tales of the North American Indians.* Bloomington: Indiana University Press, 1966.

Torrend, James. *Specimens of Bantu Folklore from Northern Rhodesia.* London: Associated Faculty Press, 1921, 1973.

ABOUT THE AUTHOR:

In addition to conducting courses for teachers and librarians who are new to storytelling or wish to hone their skills, Margaret Read MacDonald also shares her "learning-a-story-in-one-hour" techniques during weekend storytelling retreats each summer, held on Guemes Island, one of the San Juan Islands in Washington. Among other volunteer activities, the author is president of Youth Theatre Northwest and vice-president of the Seattle Storyteller's Guild.

Dr. MacDonald received her Ph.D. in folklore from Indiana University. In addition to her duties as children's librarian in the Kings County Library System in Seattle, Washington, she travels to many states to conduct minicourses in storytelling. Her books include *The Storyteller's Sourcebook, Twenty Tellable Tales, When the Lights Go Out, Booksharing,* and *The Skit Book.*